MANAGIN
CHURCH CON

GROUP THEORY APPLIED TO THE CHURCH FAMILY

by
James A. Jones

ISBN: 0-89137-558-9

Dedication

I dedicate this book to the elders of the Central Church of Christ in Dalton, Georgia. As pictured above, from left to right, they are: Troy Hogan, Lucien Claiborne, Bob Griggs, and Don Wilson.

These men have seen the need for help themselves as they have led the Central congregation. One or more have been enrolled in my counseling courses each semester since January 8, 1981. I have been greatly encouraged by their acknowledgement of needing help in dealing with people in conflict.

In June, 1982, they invited me to become a consultant to them and their ministers on a bi-monthly basis, and more frequently as needed.

Foreword

Everywhere, human beings encounter the threat and promise of groups. Wittingly or unconsciously, we find ourselves involving or detaching in relationship to groups, including family, church, community and friends. The drive to be a part of something bigger is very powerful, but for many, the fear of rejection is a more powerful determinant of one's attitude toward assemblages of important others. Whether one experiences emotional nourishment and spiritual stimulation depends on one's style of interacting and one's self-esteem. When one feels inadequate, and his style is provocative, placating or otherwise handicapping, the group leader can be an important link between the individual and the group, facilitating the individual change necessary for more secure, authentic, and rewarding interaction between the member and the group.

In this volume, James Jones examines many issues relevant to the structure and function of groups whose purpose is to afford spiritual and emotional nourishment. With scriptural correlary, he develops and explains important dynamic factors and how they interrelate. Human emotion is valued and encouraged. An attitude of Christian humility is advised for the leader. The leader is encouraged to learn about transference distortions, and make himself emotionally available to his members. He is implored not to exploit their unrealistic transference needs. He is encouraged to develop an attitude of genuine respect and interest in his group members, and lead by demonstrating this behavior in the group. The leader is admonished to make himself vulnerable to the feelings and opinions of his members. He models conflict resolution by making himself open to his members and dealing with their conflicts with him. He proves that the group can indeed weather conflict, and grow in the process. He shows that this is more desirable than sweeping things under the carpet to present a peaceful surface.

This is a book to be read more than once. On subsequent readings, it will not seem to be the same book, because it will be read from the vantage point of additional maturity; what seemed obscure the first time will make sense the second time, in the light of intervening experience in one's groups.

How rewarding to have been involved with James Jones in the preparation of this stimulating book.

Ray L. Johnson, M.D.
Clinical Assistant Professor of Psychiatry
Emory University School of Medicine

TABLE OF CONTENTS

Dedication iii
Foreword iv
Introduction ix
Preface xi
Acknowledgments xiii

CHAPTER ONE

How Do I Fit in a Group?

1. A Person Needs a Group 1
2. Why Does an Individual Become a Member of a Group? 1
3. To Understand Groups, One Must Understand Symbols 2
4. Three Models of Group Development 2
5. A Group Communicates on Several Levels Simultaneously 8
6. What Affects One Member Affects Every Member 9
7. How Pain Is Manifested in the Group 9
8. How Do I Fit in a Group? 13

CHAPTER TWO

Conflict Is Inherent in Any Group.

1. Conflict Has Been, and Will Be, in the Church 17
2. There Are Some Conflicts Which Can Be Prevented 17
3. There Are Some Conflicts Which Are Unhealthy 19
4. Some Conflicts Are Healthy 26
5. Nine Interrelated Reasons Why Some Conflicts May Never Be Resolved 27

CHAPTER THREE

Are Group Norms a Defense Against or a Reflection of Self?

1. What Are the Rules? 31
2. The Bible—A Defense Against Growth or a Guide to Self-Discovery and Growth 31
3. Performance of Acts (Rituals) Can Be a Vehicle Into or Away From Self 33
4. Avenues of Worship—Defense Mechanisms or Means of Self-Revelation, Self-Expression, and Self-Growth 34

5. What Are Defense Mechanisms, and Why Are They Necessary? 34
6. Common Defense Mechanisms Which a Person Uses to Protect Himself 36
7. The Value of a Contract 40

CHAPTER FOUR

There Cannot Be Conflict Without Emotions.

1. What One Feels About Feelings Makes It Easier or More Difficult to Accept Feelings 43
2. Feelings Are Friends, Not Enemies 44
3. Understanding One's Heart 45
4. All Group Members Have the Right to Have Their Feelings as Well as to Experience Them 46
5. All Group Members Have the Right to Feel the Feelings They Have Toward Other Group Members 47
6. All Group Members Have the Right to Express Their Feelings Verbally and Nonverbally 48
7. All Group Members Have the Right to Listen and Respond to the Feelings the Other Group Members Are or Are Not Sharing 50
8. All Group Members Have the Right to Process or Work Through Their Feelings 53

CHAPTER FIVE

What Should We Do With Our Anger?

1. Leaders and Followers Get Angry 60
2. A Leader Needs to Recognize and Label His Anger As Anger—Not Call It Something Else 60
3. A Leader Needs to Know the Cause of His Anger 62
4. Frustration Is a Cause of Anger 64
5. Unrealistic View of Self and Others Causes Anger 64
6. Jealousy Is a Cause of Anger 65
7. Impatience Causes Anger 70
8. Several Other Causes of Anger 70
9. What a Leader Should Do About Anger in Himself 71
10. How Should a Leader Respond to Anger in Group Members? 72

CHAPTER SIX

The Art of Listening Is Inherent in the Art of Leading.

1. Listening Is Needed 77

2. Listening Helps the Group to Prevent and Resolve Conflicts . . . 77
3. Members Are Not Made for Programs—Programs Should Be Made for Members . . . 78
4. Why Do Leaders Not Listen? . . . 80
5. A Leader May Not Listen to a Person or Group Because He Feels Afraid, Ashamed, or Guilty About His Own Feelings . . . 81
6. A Leader May Not Listen to Feelings Because He Thinks They Are Not Important . . . 85
7. A Leader May Not Listen Because He Does Not Want to Get Involved with Another Person . . . 86
8. A Leader May Not Listen Because He Is Too Preoccupied with His Own Problems, Too Involved in Other Matters, or Too Tired . . . 90
9. A Leader May Not Listen to Others Because He Is Afraid of Criticism . . . 95
10. A Leader May Not Listen Because He Has Closed His Eyes, Ears and Heart, and Therefore Has Become Hard-Headed and Hard-Hearted . . . 98
11. A Leader May Not Listen Because He Does Not Know How to Listen . . . 99

CHAPTER SEVEN

A Leader May Need to Be a God.
1. Everyone Uses Some of the Following Tactics to Some Degree at One Time or Another . . . 103
2. Some Things Which Influence a Person to Think He Is a God . . . 103
3. Dedication Should Not Be Confused with Obsession . . . 104
4. A Leader Who Needs to Be a God Thinks He Is Omniscient . . . 105
5. A Leader Who Needs to Be a God Thinks He Is Omnipotent . . . 106
6. A Leader Who Needs to Be a God Is Certainly Grandiose . . . 108
7. A Leader Who Needs to Be a God Avoids Feelings . . . 108
8. A Leader Who Needs to Be a God Is Stubborn . . . 110
9. A Leader Who Needs to Be a God Operates More by Fear than by Faith . . . 110
10. A Leader Who Needs to Be a God Thinks He Is Perfect . . . 111
11. A Leader Who Needs to Be a God Cannot Experience Complete Forgiveness . . . 112

CHAPTER EIGHT

Reasons Why Members Need Their Leaders to Be Gods.

1. The God Symbol 117
2. Infantile Members Need to See Their Leaders as Gods 118
3. Insecurity, Anxiety, and Confusion Cause Members to See Their Leaders as Gods 119
4. A Person Behaves Differently in a Group..............119
5. Who Has the Power in This Group? 122

CHAPTER NINE

Qualities of an Effective Leader.

1. Traits Are Interrelated 125
2. An Effective Group Leader Is Not Controlled by His Past 125
3. An Effective Leader Understands Group Dynamics 127
4. An Effective Leader Understands Transference and Countertransference 129
5. An Effective Leader Analyzes Resistance and Transference 137
6. An Effective Leader Sees the Group as a Recapitulation of One's Family 141

A Challenge to Christian Leaders 143

Introduction

During the course of a person's lifetime, he will be a member of different groups for various reasons. An individual who is maturing learns that he can get different needs met in different groups. This depends upon such factors as the type of leader, group norms, goals, and its size. The goals of a large religious group are not the same as those of a small psychotherapy group. Both groups can have meaning for a person, but he should not expect to get his needs met in the same manner, nor to the same degree, in both groups.

The dynamics interrelate in all groups, but the degree of intimacy and self-disclosure vary considerably. A person will not experience intimacy in a large group because of its size and the fact that the environment in such a group is not safe. Intimacy is experienced through mutual sharing which is based on trust, acceptance, concern, respect, and responsibility. What would be appropriate for a person to share in one group would be inappropriate to share in another. Behavior which is appropriate in one group would be unacceptable in another.

This book is an introduction to some of the dynamics which are active in a group. As an introduction, its design has been to point the reader in the direction of understanding group dynamics and group process. Therefore, it was not written with the intention of being comprehensive and exhaustive. Critical, academic, and clinical research has gone into forming the bases for this book. Although it is a brief introduction written on a nontechnical level, the concepts are based on sound group theory.

Families and congregations do not have an option as to whether there will be conflict in either group. Some conflict can be prevented, but it is only an illusion to think there will be no conflict in either the church family or the nuclear family. Leaders and group members alike would experience less frustration and exasperation if they became committed to learning how to manage conflict effectively instead of holding to a false assumption. In addition, the energy spent to perpetuate an illusion could be used creatively to prevent degeneration and promote growth.

Since both the nuclear family and the local church family are groups, ignorance of group dynamics is not a viable option for those leaders who are committed to nurturing their members. Although leaders may be interested in **managing** group conflict without feeling a need to **understand** group dynamics, effective management of group conflict requires insight into how to deal with the powerful forces within a group. This book gives an indication of what some of these forces are and how to manage them effectively.

The masculine pronoun is consistently used throughout the book for the sake of brevity. It is meant to denote humankind rather than the male gender; therefore, it is hoped that its use will not be offensive to female readers.

Although the people pictured in the illustrations in this book are lifelike, they are not intentional representations of any person, living or dead, known to either Virginia Richardson or myself. Thus, any resemblance to actual persons is purely coincidental.

August 17, 1984
James A. Jones
Atlanta, Georgia

Preface

"If they don't listen to me, I'm going to take my contribution and go somewhere else."

"I think it would be a good idea for you to resign your job as preacher of this congregation during the services today."

"I'll bust this congregation wide open, if I have to, to keep it sound in the faith."

These are a few of the many statements that I have heard that remind me that conflict is still in the church nineteen hundred years this side of the murmuring of Grecians against the Hebrews in the early days of the first congregation in Jerusalem. In fact, conflict is normal—in the church, in a family, and inside a specific individual.

Since I have learned this, my goal has not been to eliminate or avoid all conflict, but to minimize all that is possible and to handle well the rest.

In this book, James Jones addresses, in a very biblical and practical way, attitudes and actions that are helpful in managing conflict in the church.

I have been closely associated with James for the past two and one-half years. He served as a part-time staff member for a year as Minister of Family Life at the Central church of Christ, Dalton, Georgia, where I am pulpit minister. During that year, he taught classes on Parenting, Managing Family Conflict, The Bible and Mental Health, and The Seasons of Our Lives. Since January, 1982, he has spent each Monday in Dalton, in private practice as a marriage and family therapist. On Monday nights, he has taught a three-hour college-level class in counseling. I feel that I have learned and grown from each class in which I have participated.

During the time that we have worked together, I have had the opportunity to refer to James a number of individuals and families with whom I had been counseling. I have been an observer in many of these sessions. James Jones puts into practice what he teaches in his classes and writes in his books.

Perhaps some of his most effective work with the Central congregation has been as a consultant. In this role, he does not tell the staff or elders what to do or how to "run" the church. But rather, as we meet with him twice each month on a regular basis, as an interested and trained "outsider" (he and his family live and worship in the Atlanta area), he leads us in thinking and evaluating different ways of dealing with problems that arise, such as difficult family problems in the congregation, elder-staff-congregation communication, and the most effective way to work through the process of church discipline.

I have read and recommended his previous books, *Counseling Principles for Christian Leaders* and *I Never Thought It Would Be This Way*. He has also contributed three chapters to the book *Growing Through Conflict*. All these volumes are published by Quality Publications. Since I have read the manuscript for this book, *Managing Church Conflict*, I have been encouraging brethren to get a copy.

Elders, preachers, deacons, and all Christians who would like to be able to better understand the relationships in the group God calls His church will do well to read, study, and discuss the information in this book.

I have found very helpful the insight I have gained in this book relating to the following questions:

- When is conflict healthy?
- What are some principles for resolving conflict?
- What are the causes of anger, and how can I handle it?
- Why do some leaders find it difficult, if not impossible, to listen?

Since knowing James Jones and reading this book, I gladly commend him and it for your learning and growth.

—Jerrie W. Barber
Central church of Christ
Dalton, Georgia
August 3, 1984

Acknowledgements

In a number of ways, this book is the result of a group effort. While I take responsibility for writing the book, it could not have been written without the help of others.

I am grateful to Nancy Browne, Joan Scraggs and Barbara Walker for their help in preparing the rough draft of the manuscript. I appreciate Sherrel Wilson for typing some of the initial drafts. I am indebted to Howard J. McDonald for typing two complete drafts. Without his patience and persistence, this book would not have been completed.

Virginia Richardson designed the cover and drew the illustrations for each chapter. It is with gratitude that I acknowledge the significant contribution which her artwork adds to understanding the message of this book.

I express my deep gratitude to Jerrie Barber, Ray Loring Johnson, M.D., and Gretchen Webb for reading the manuscript and making valuable suggestions. I further acknowledge my appreciation to Jerrie for writing the preface and to Ray for writing the foreword.

To Tom Byerley, an elder of the Hillcrest church of Christ in Atlanta, Georgia, I express my gratitude for the encouragement he has given me through the years. Thus, indirectly he has helped to make this book possible. Tom has seen the need for elders to be trained in helping people solve their problems and live less stressful lives. He has been willing to become a student himself. He began taking my counseling courses in January, 1981, and is currently enrolled in his eighth semester.

1 *How Do I Fit In A Group?*

"... you too are being built together to become a dwelling in which God lives by his spirit."

(Ephesians 2:22)

A Person Needs a Group

One of the strongest needs of man is to belong to a group. In fact, a person comes into this world as a result of two individuals having been at least physically related, and no one lives to himself alone or dies to himself alone (Romans 14:7). Thus, relationships are necessary for man's beginning, and they significantly influence who he becomes as he journeys through life.

Groups (religious and secular) can have a positive or negative influence on an individual. In fact, Paul said, "Do not be misled: 'Bad company corrupts good character' " (1 Corinthians 15:33). He further stated, "Therefore, encourage one another and build each other up, just as in fact you are doing" (1 Thessalonians 5:11). Solomon said, "My son, if sinners entice you, do not give in to them" (Proverbs 1:10).

A person needs to belong to a group in order to have his needs met, and will therefore be attracted to different groups throughout his life. Of course, the first group to which a person belongs is his family. As an individual matures, though, he will likely become a member of different groups (for example, school, sports, peer, church, business, political, etc.) for various reasons.

Why Does an Individual Become a Member of a Group?

A person becomes a member of a group to meet personal and social needs. A group becomes meaningful to him to the degree that his needs are met in it. When an individual does not have his needs met in ways which are satisfactory, the group will cease to be important to him. The time this takes can vary from weeks to months and even years. An individual may not leave the group because of fear, guilt, and/or embarrassment, but he may very well become apathetic. It is important to understand that a person can become confused about himself and how to have his needs met. Isaiah said, "Woe to those who call evil good and good evil, who put darkness for light and light for darkness, who put bitter for sweet and sweet for bitter" (Isaiah 5:20). The fact remains that if a person's needs are not met in one group (family, church, etc.), he will seek another. There are some personal needs which do not change with age (for example, to belong and be meaningfully related to significant others), although the way in which they are met does. There are some personal needs which will change as one matures. These include developmental, educational, marital, family, and professional needs. This being the case, the church has a tremendously complex responsibility.

To Understand Groups, One Must Understand Symbols

In order to understand groups and effectively function in them, it is imperative for a person to **learn** to **think symbolically** as well as to make **skillful and appropriate use of symbols**. This means that a person must grow in his **metaphorical** thinking and freely associate current experiences and circumstances with similar ones in his past.

Symbols are necessary to the discovery of and participation in the unconscious. Symbols can penetrate members' defenses and open them up to areas of themselves to which they may be blind. Furthermore, a symbol can be less threatening to an individual than direct confrontation.

An individual who effectively responds to group dynamics does so out of insight into the multi-level communication which is always taking place within a group. Multi-level communication has reference to verbal and nonverbal, intellectual and emotional, conscious and unconscious components of what is or is not said. Therefore, a person must train himself to listen on different levels simultaneously while thinking metaphorically or analogously. This art can be learned, but not without considerable analytical thinking and persistent effort.

Three Models of Group Development

Through the years, groups have been studied from many different angles. Research shows that there are essentially three basic models of group development (Kellerman, 1981). These models are useful in studying group dynamics and group process. A model which I use is based on an integration of the following three models: the linear progressive model, the pendular or recurring cycle model, and the life cycle model.

The **linear progressive model** is one in which a group develops in a progressive way toward its stated goal. Tuckman (1965) sees a group as moving through four stages, which are as follows:

(1) **Testing** is a dependency stage. In this stage, the group members test the leader and, to some degree, each other regarding authority issues, nature and structure of the group, and norms and goals.

(2) **Storming** is the initial conflict stage. The group fights over such issues as the leader, the leader's authority, and the problems they have relating to him and to each other.

(3) **Norming** is the stage which reflects a resolution of conflict and the harmonious emergence of roles.

(4) **Performing** is the stage in which the group performs its tasks in an attempt to reach its goal.

Bennis and Shepard (1974) give two major stages of group development. The first is the **authority-dependency** phase, which has three subphases:

(1) **Dependency-flight** is the subphase in which group life is filled with behavior in which the remote and immediate aims are to ward off anxiety. Much of the discussion involves searching for a common goal. There is considerable security-seeking behavior in which members reassure one another through sharing interesting and harmless facts about themselves. Some idiosyncratic behavior occurs in the form of doodles, yawns, and intellectualizations.

(2) **Counterdependency-fight** is the subphase in which a leader fails to satisfy the needs of the group, and thus counterdependent expressions begin to replace overt dependency. In some ways, this phase is the most stressful and unpleasant in the life of the group. It is a paradoxical development of a leader's role into one of omnipotence on

the one hand and powerlessness on the other hand. It is also characterized by the group's dividing into warring subgroups. In subphase one, feelings of hostility were strongly defended. Even if a slip were made which suggested hostility, especially towards the leader, the group members would be embarrassed. In this subphase, expressions of hostility are more frequent and are more likely to be endorsed by other members. Power is more overtly the concern of group members. The discussion of power (leadership) is no longer about dependency on the leader, but about how he has failed as a leader.

(3) In order to understand the **resolution-catharsis** subphase one must understand the types of group members as discussed by Bennis and Shepard. Group members who find comfort in rules of procedure, an agenda, or an expert are designated as **dependent**. Those group members who are uncomfortable with authoritative structures are called **counterdependent**. Members who insist on having a relatively high degree of intimacy with all the others are designated as being **overpersonal**. Members who tend to avoid intimacy are called **counterpersonal**. Members who assume compulsively highly dependent, highly counterdependent, highly personal, or highly counterpersonal roles are designated as **conflicted**. These individuals tend not to learn from their experiences because they are not aware of, nor in control of the components of their conflict. For example, a person who is very submissive is most likely a person who lacks genuine trust or who is rebellious. It is the existence of conflict which accounts for dramatic movement from extreme dependency to extreme rebelliousness at times in a group. Members who are **unconflicted** or **independent** are better able to profit from their experiences and to assess the present situation more accurately. Naturally, they may act in rebellious or submissive ways at times. Members who are capable of reducing the uncertainty characterizing a given phase are called **catalysts, initiators**, or **central persons** (Redl, 1942).

In this subphase, the resolution of the group's difficulties depends upon group forces which have, until this time, been inoperative or ineffective. The leader has no magic and is powerless. His contributions only serve to solidify the subgroups. Remember, the group is formed into subgroups, with the exception of the **independents** who have not developed firm bonds with warring subgroups. The independents are the only hope for survival since they have thus far avoided polarization and stereotypic behavior. The leadership they provide (the group does not see them as having vested interest and power) leads to resolution of conflict and catharsis.

The second phase is the **interdependency phase**, in which conflict regarding authority-dependency issues has been essentially worked through. The group moves more into interpersonal issues.

(4) In the beginning of subphase four, which is the **enchantment-flight subphase**, the group is happy, cohesive, and relaxed. The effects of fighting are still fresh in the memory of the group, and therefore any tension is responded to through jokes and laughter. The group attempts to heal wounds, superficially work out differences, and maintain a harmonious atmosphere. There is considerable merrymaking, but the pleasures begin to wear thin relatively soon.

The group tries to perpetuate the myth of mutual acceptance and universal harmony, but from the beginning of this subphase, there are indications of underlying hostilities and unresolved issues in the group. Although this subphase begins with catharsis, the group soon develops a rigid norm to which all members are forced to conform. In effect, this rule reads as follows: "Nothing must be allowed to disturb our harmony in the future; we must avoid the mistakes of the painful past." The members really have not forgotten that it was the past which brought them to their delightful present. Instead, they choose to carefully overlook their past experiences.

Gradually the group members begin resisting the requirement that harmony be maintained at all costs. In open discussion, no member dares endanger the harmony by denying that all problems have been solved. The flight from these problems manifests itself in various ways. The group members who have resolved not to fight may also think that further self-study is unnecessary. One common way of preventing the group from dealing with its problems is that of dividing into subgroups or committees and not meeting as a total group. Individuals may begin to behave in ways alien to their own feelings. They may think that to go still further in group involvement would result in a complete loss of self. Thus, the group may start emphasizing that they love one another and must maintain the solidarity of the group, and give up whatever is necessary of their selfish desires. An individual may begin thinking that he has to sacrifice his own identity as a person to support the group. The joy and excitement at the beginning of the subphase is maintained only as a mask toward the end. The group members would like the leader once again to take over.

(5) In subphase five, which is the **disenchantment-fight phase**, the group again experiences dynamics similar to that of subphase two. Only this time, the subgroups are warring over the degree of intimacy required by group membership. The overpersonal members want unconditional love, while the counterpersonal members resist further involvement. Subphase five belongs to the counterpersonals as subphase four belonged to the overpersonals. This is the first time openly disparaging remarks are made about the group. The overpersonal members insist they are happy and comfortable, while the counterpersonal members complain about lack of group morale. The overpersonal members intellectualize in religious overtones about Christian love and caring for others. The counterpersonal members explain behavior in terms of motives which have nothing to do with the present group. The overpersonals explain behavior in terms of acceptance and rejection in the present group.

(6) Through the dynamic processes, the group moves into subphase six, which is **consensual validation**. The main work of the group during this subphase is that of each group member verbalizing his personal conceptual scheme for understanding human behavior. This level of work necessitates skill in communication. Some important realizations from the group's work during this subphase are as follows:

(a) Individual differences are accepted and not seen as

good or bad.

(b) The conflict which exists is over substantive issues instead of emotional issues.

(c) Consensus is reached through rational discussion, not through a compulsive attempt at unanimity.

(d) Members are aware of their involvement and other aspects of group process, without being overwhelmed.

(e) Through the evaluation process, members become more meaningful to each other. This process also facilitates communication and creates a deeper understanding of what the other person thinks, how he feels, and how he behaves. As a result, personal expectations emerge which are to be distinguished from the previous more stereotyped role expectations.

The central problems of group life are dependency and interdependency, power and love, authority and intimacy. The evolution of the group represents a change from power to affection, and from role to personality.

Kaplan (1967) develops a three-phase phenomenon with a linear model. He sees these phases as being dependency, power, and intimacy. In this initial phase, the group is dependent. As the group matures, it must learn how to manage power, concerns, and struggles. When these issues are resolved, the group may mature to the point of intimacy.

Kellerman (1979) gives a linear model which is called "regressive" or "retrogressive." According to Kellerman, the first competitive stage leads to a power struggle. The group then moves to a control versus acting-out stage. As the group matures, it reaches a dependency stage. These stages correspond to Freud's theory of the psychosexual development of a person, indicating that the group retrogresses from the oedipal through the phallic to the oral stage.

The **pendular** or **recurring cycle model** is one in which an oscillation between issues occurs throughout the life of the group. One way of measuring the growth of the group is to note whether there has been movement (forward or backward) when old issues emerge. This model stresses the evolution of boundaries (Mills, 1964), which the group members both fear and desire.

The **life-cycle model** emphasizes the birth, development, and death of the group. Major emphasis is given to the death of the group. This model suggests that the group goes through the same developmental stages as an individual does. A leader who understands the developmental stages of a person can, upon observing a group, determine its present stage of development.

Another way of viewing groups is to see them as having a life cycle which is analogous to one's family. Of course, a family is a group. The dynamics which are present in the formation and development of the group are similar to those which go into the making and development of a family. In fact, a group is a recapitulation of one's primary family group (Yalom, 1975).

A Group Communicates on Several Levels Simultaneously

Group members communicate verbally and nonverbally, intellectually and emotionally, consciously and unconsciously through what is said as well as what is not said. **Group members are saying something about themselves and what is happening within the group regardless of the topic being discussed**. When the members are talking about **things outside the group**, they are talking about **things within the group**. Granted, their talking may be to avoid (consciously or unconsciously) what is really going on within themselves and between the members. Solomon said, "Even in laughter the heart may ache, and joy may end in grief" (Proverbs 14:13). John recorded, "You say, 'I am rich; I have acquired wealth and do not need a thing.' But you do not realize that you are wretched, pitiful, poor, blind and naked" (Revelation 3:17).

A person cannot understand the meaning of his words without understanding them **experientially**. In fact most, if not all, communication has a present and past element which is rooted in one's feelings. Percentagewise, more people listen to understand the words an individual is saying than to understand the feelings (or lack of them) through which another communicates. What a person verbalizes is minor compared to what and how he expresses himself emotionally while saying the words. An individual can use his words to communicate or avoid expressing his feelings. A person's current feelings may also be rooted in his past experiences.

An individual who persistently uses words (intellectualizes) to avoid his emotions (current or past) automatically limits his degree of involvement in the group. He also influences the type of problems with which the group can deal. If the group has a dominant person (especially the leader) who communicates primarily on an intellectual level, then the emotional aspects of their conflicts cannot be properly addressed or solved. The group's pain cannot be reached, much less dealt with, through intellectualization. In fact, intellectualizing is an effective means through which the group avoids its pain.

What Affects One Member Affects Every Member

Regarding the body (group), Paul said, "...its parts should have equal concern for each other. If one part suffers, every part suffers with it; if one part is honored, every part rejoices with it" (1 Corinthians 12:25,26). **Pain** and **conflict** are inherent in the nature and development of a group. The same forces which can be constructive can also be destructive. The way in which a group manages its conflicts and processes its pains largely determines whether the group will grow or degenerate. Neither individuals nor the group remain the same, although **resistance** to growth is a way of trying to maintain **sameness**.

How Pain Is Manifested in the Group

There are **different types** and **degrees** of **pain**. Some is caused by external circumstances and some by internal conflicts which may be healthy or pathological. The nature, complexity, and intensity of the pain determines the treatment. For example, some pain requires first aid, some emergency aid, and some hospitalization, major surgery, prolonged complicated treatment, and a longer period of time for recovery. Wise indeed are the leaders who accurately differentiate between types of pain and are skilled enough to treat properly and/or call in a consultant. Making an accurate diagnosis, and developing and implementing a realistic and adequate treatment plan are perhaps where most leaders need improvement.

How members manifest their personal pain and the group's pain is not always obvious. Nevertheless, it is easy to see some pain. For example, Paul said, "Recalling your tears, I long to see you, so that I may be filled with joy" (2 Timothy 1:4). Where and how the group's pain is manifested becomes an important question to one who seeks insight into group dynamics and the methods of responding effectively to them. There are several interrelated ways through which the group's pain is manifested.

Pain is present when members feel they **do not belong** or **fit with** each other. Paul said:

> *Now the body is not made up of one part but of many. If the foot should say, "Because I am not a hand, I do not belong to the body," it would not for that reason cease to be part of the body. And if the ear should say, "Because I am not an eye, I do not belong to the body," it would not for that reason cease to be part of the body. If the whole body were an eye, where would the sense of hearing be? If the whole body were an ear, where would the sense of smell be? But in fact God has arranged the parts in the body, every one of them, just as he wanted them to be. If they were all one part, where would the body be? As it is, there are many parts, but one body (1 Corinthians 12:14-20).*

A person's use of pronouns indicates whether he feels he fits into the group. When an individual uses **they** and **them** to refer to **his** group instead of **we, us**, or **our**, then he does not feel that he belongs or fits. Obviously, he could use **we, us**, and **our** and not feel that he belongs, but he would probably not do this frequently. Feeling that one fits or belongs is not a fixed state or condition, but is a dynamic process. Therefore, when an individual and/or the group is changing (whether by growth or degeneration), there will be times when one **does not fit**—and this is **painful**. When this does happen, though, adequate attention should be given immediately to those affected. The quicker pain is specifically diagnosed and adequately treated, the less deterioration occurs and the faster healing takes place. Thus, the affected member and the group can move on to other creative functions.

Pain is present when **members pretend they do not need each other**. When this is the case, obviously they do not feel as though they fit or belong in a deep sense. Paul said:

> *The eye cannot say to the hand, "I don't need you!" And the head cannot say to the feet, "I don't need you!" On the contrary, those parts of the body that seem to be weaker are indispensable, and the parts that we think are less honorable we treat with special honor. And the parts that are unpresentable are treated with special modesty, while our presentable parts need no special treatment. But God has combined the members of the body and has given greater honor to the parts that lacked it, so that there should be no division in the body, but that its parts should have equal concern for each other. If one part suffers, every part suffers with it; if one part is honored, every part rejoices with it (1 Corinthians 12:21-26).*

Denial of needing each other may lead members to rigidity, authoritarianism, withdrawal, apathy, and depression. In attempting to cope with their pain, the group members may utilize other defense mechanisms.

Being absent from or **arriving late** to group meetings are ways members can express feeling that they do not fit in the group. Such behavior can also communicate their anger and may be an attempt to deny their need of each other. Sitting in the back of the room can be a way through which a member expresses his fear of the group and/or the feeling that he does not belong. When members **deny** their need for each other, their pain becomes blocked. Thus, they cannot share deeply in each other's suffering or rejoicing, even though Paul exhorted the Romans to "rejoice with those who rejoice; mourn with those who mourn" (Romans 12:15). This condition naturally leads to **loneliness**, which is a **manifestation of the group member's pain**.

Loneliness has both intrapersonal and interpersonal dimensions which are interrelated. When one is experiencing loneliness, he is also experiencing a broken relationship (with jagged edges) with himself, others, and/or God. When one is lonely, he experiences other feelings.

Loneliness is a painful sensation of emptiness and a deeply hollow throbbing ache which varies in intensity and duration. It is a feeling of frustration which comes from a need to be related on various levels to oneself and others. It is a feeling of being cut off and isolated from oneself and/or meaningful others. Thus, one experiences feelings of loss, and even confusion.

Sometimes loneliness is experienced because one is not aware of what he needs and how to be related to himself and/or others in a way through which his needs can be met. Sometimes loneliness is experienced because one needs to be symbiotically related (becoming one with another) in areas where the two cannot (for whatever reasons—time, tiredness, unwillingness, fear, ignorance, etc.) be so related. Sometimes loneliness is experienced because one is attempting to meet earlier developmental needs with inappropriate persons.

Men and women often marry spouses who remind them of their parents (either consciously or unconsciously), or they may relate to another group member as to a parent. When this occurs, the individual may experience much isolation and loneliness, because spouses and group members cannot, in fact, be parents to each other. They may attempt parenting for a while and experience some relatedness, even symbiosis; but the reality of marriage, having children, and personal growth will eventually interrupt the symbiosis and will likely produce considerable feelings of isolation and loneliness.

An individual needs to be related to himself and others intimately on various levels, such as intellectually, emotionally, and spiritually. He even needs intimacy which is of such depths that the two become one. A person may desire continuous oneness in every area of his personal and social needs. This inevitably will produce loneliness because, in reality, it is impossible. An individual may have a deep-seated desire for continuous intimacy because the thought of functioning separately from the other raises intense anxiety or a feeling of being abandoned. Anxiety which is rooted in a feeling of being abandoned is also rooted in earlier parent-child relationships. It suggests that a person had difficulty in separating from his parents (especially his mother) and becoming his own person. The individual who, in fact, has the ego strength or is mature enough to be creatively involved in therapeutic relationships (for example, personal and group therapy) can process his residual separation/individuation issues and learn how to be a person who can be intimately related to himself and others.

Leaders who need to be **gods** actually contribute to loneliness when they promise a person, at least by implication, that by being affiliated with them, the individual's needs will be met continuously and that the group functions as **one** at all times. These expectations are especially likely to cause loneliness in the individual who is unaware of his unresolved separation/individuation issues.

One's loneliness is more intense and its duration longer the more he needs a person or particular group (like his family or church) to meet all of his needs. This suggests that he has residual separation/individuation issues which have not been adequately and therapeutically processed. The individual who has essentially resolved the separation/individuation issues will experience loneliness when he is cut off (for whatever reasons) from himself and important others, but his loneliness will tend to be less intense and less lasting, because becoming related to himself and others on the levels he needs is less complicated. In addition, not having to deal with earlier developmental needs which were not met satisfactorily will require less time for him once again to become related.

How Do I Fit in a Group?

How one fits in a group is contingent upon a number of factors, such as the type of leader, the nature of the group, and the individual himself. A skilled leader is concerned with helping the group develop in areas which will enable each member to feel that he belongs and can grow in this group.

In an open group (one which receives new members), an effective leader is interested in helping a group become aware of **its resistance** to accepting new members. Even a group which is open for new members resists receiving them. There are many reasons why they resist, and five are as follows:

(1) Adding even one new member changes the make-up of the group, and therefore is disruptive to some degree.

(2) One new member forces the group to change.

(3) Change is painful, and therefore the group resists.

(4) In order for a group to accept a new member, it must regress and again go through the developmental stages.

(5) Regression is painful and requires work, and thus the group resists.

If a new member is to fit, he must want to fit, and the group must accept responsibility for processing its resistance to his becoming a part of the group. Becoming a member of a group requires mutual desire and acceptance of both the individual and the group.

References

Bennis, W. G., and Shepard, H. A., "A Theory of Group Development;" Gibbard, G. S., Hartman, J. J., and Mann, R. D. (Eds.), **Analysis of Groups** (San Francisco: Jossey-Bass, 1974).

Kaplan, S. R., "Therapy Groups and Training Groups: Similarities and Differences;" **International Journal of Group Psychotherapy**, 1967, **171**, 473-504.

Kellerman, H., **Group Cohesion: Theoretical and Clinical Perspectives** (New York: Grune and Stratton, 1981).

Kellerman, H., **Group Psychotherapy and Personality: Intersecting Structures** (New York: Grune and Stratton, 1979).

Mills, T. M., **Group Transformation: An Analysis of a Learning Group** (Englewood Cliff, New Jersey: Prentice Hall, 1964).

Redl, F., "Group Emotion and Leadership;" **Psychiatry**, 1942, **5**, 573-596.

Tuckmann, B., "Developmental Sequence in Small Groups;" **Psychological Bulletin**, 1965, **631**, 384-399.

Yalom, I. D., **The Theory and Practice of Group Psychotherapy** (New York: Basic Books, Inc., 1975 [2nd edition]).

2 *Conflict Is Inherent In Any Group.*

"If one part suffers, every part suffers with it: if one part is honored, every part rejoices with it."

(1 Corinthians 12:26)

Conflict Has Been and Will Be in the Church

Conflict has been experienced by individuals since Adam and Eve. It has been in the church at least since Acts, chapter six. Conflict is in the church today, and it will be in the church tomorrow. Some conflict can be prevented, and some is unhealthy. The fact remains, though, that conflict is inherent in meeting personal and group needs. When conflict emerges as a result of growth (personal or group) or in an attempt to grow, it is natural and potentially healthy for the individual and the group. Thus, **growth-oriented conflict,** if managed properly, is **hopeful,** and is **a sign of spirituality**.

There Are Some Conflicts Which Can Be Prevented

Some conflicts can be prevented if the individuals involved genuinely **accept** the fact that **personal and group conflict is inevitable**. Failure on the part of the group to accept this fact will contribute to unnecessary conflict. This deception influences members to use denial as a defense mechanism to keep them from facing conflict when it emerges. Conflict is dynamic; therefore, the longer it is avoided in continuing relationships, the more it grows.

Some conflicts can be prevented if the **group has planned realistically** and **adequately** for **conflict resolution** or **management** once it emerges. In many congregations there are no plans, much less realistic and adequate ones, for resolving or managing conflict. I have heard leaders in congregations say for years such ridiculous things as "Christians should just get along" or "We're Christians," as though Christians are not people, or the trite and false statement that "Christians don't have problems; they only have opportunities." No one with average intelligence would dare think, much less say, that a surgeon should wait until he has a patient to study how to do surgery. Yet, in some elderships and congregations, there are no adequate plans for dealing with conflict once it emerges.

Some conflicts can be prevented if the group members accept that when conflict emerges, it **does not** necessarily mean that the persons involved are **guilty of sin** or that **they will sin by confronting it.** Group leaders and members need to perceive clearly that conflict is inherent in being both an individual and a member of a group. Conflict in and of itself is not sinful. The ones who are in conflict may sin by the way they respond to each other verbally and nonverbally, but conflict in itself is not sinful.

If individuals think they will sin by confronting conflict, they most likely will tend to deny the conflict or try to avoid the conflictual issues. Obviously, group members can sin through the way they respond to conflict, but confronting it **per se** is not sinful. It is the way in which conflict is confronted, not the confrontation itself, which may be sinful.

Some conflicts can be prevented if the group members have **realistic expectations of themselves.** Many conflicts emerge because the group members have expectations of themselves which just are not realistic. Some of their expectations are as follows:

(1) We should like each other all of the time and never dislike one another.

(2) We should always smile and be in a good mood.

(3) We should always be joyful and never sad.

(4) We should always be in agreement with each other and never disagree with one another—especially the leaders.

(5) We should always be on the mountain peak and never in the valley of the mountain, or we should always be up and never down.

(6) We should always count our assets (blessings) and never our liabilities (problems or conflicts).

(7) We should be idealistic, not realistic.

These and other types of unrealistic expectations create unnecessary conflict.

Some conflicts can be prevented if the leaders and the group members set **realistic and achievable goals** for themselves. They must then **focus** on the **process of achieving them instead of focusing on the goals themselves.** Conflict within the group may arise from a failure to set goals, or it may result from the setting of unrealistic goals. Also, conflict may emerge as a result of focusing only on the goals instead of on the means to achieve them.

Some conflicts can be prevented if each member learns how to **mind his own business.** Considerable conflict may result from a member focusing on another instead of learning to think and speak for himself. Paul said, "Make it your ambition to lead a quiet life, to mind your own business and to work with your hands, just as we told you, so that your daily life may win the respect of outsiders and so that you will not be dependent on anybody" (1 Thessalonians 4:11,12). Solomon spoke to this issue when he said, "Like one who seizes a dog by the ears is a passer-by who meddles in a quarrel not his own" (Proverbs 26:17).

It becomes very important, therefore, in the prevention and resolution of conflict, for the members to **differentiate the dimensions of conflict.** There are at least three dimensions to any conflict. They are intrapersonal, interpersonal, and objective. **Intrapersonal conflict** has reference to the struggle within the individual group member. **Interpersonal conflict** refers to the conflict between individuals within the group. The **objective dimension** of conflict concerns the facts of reality within the group, or those objective matters about which the group is in conflict; for example, changes in agenda, frequency of meeting, or inappropriate behavior of a member.

There Are Some Conflicts Which Are Unhealthy

A conflict is unhealthy if it is the result of the members **accusing, blaming, and ridiculing** each other, or if they take this approach in trying to resolve an otherwise healthy conflict.

A conflict is unhealthy if it results from **trivia** and **not substance.** In any group there will be conflict at times over trivia, but unless the group matures to a level where trivia is given up and their conflict is over substance, their conflicts will be unhealthy. Another way of expressing the same concept is that group members must grow to the point where they differentiate their opinions from matters of faith.

A conflict is unhealthy if the members are **arguing about words** and engaging in **godless chatter** to avoid the deeper intrapersonal and interpersonal components of their conflict. Paul addressed this matter when he said:

Keep reminding them of these things. Warn them before God against quarreling about words; it is of no value, and only ruins those who listen. Do your best to present yourself to God as one approved, a workman who does not need to be ashamed and who correctly handles the word of truth. Avoid godless chatter, because those who indulge in it will become more and more ungodly. Their teaching will spread like gangrene...Don't have anything to do with foolish and stupid arguments, because you know they produce quarrels. And the Lord's servant must not quarrel; instead, he must be kind to everyone, able to teach, not resentful. Those who oppose him he must gently instruct, in the hope that God will give them a change of heart leading them to a knowledge of the truth, and that they will come to their senses and escape from the trap of the devil, who has taken them captive to do his will (2 Timothy 2:14-17, 23-26).

But avoid foolish controversies and genealogies and arguments and quarrels about the law, because these are unprofitable and useless. Warn a divisive person once, and then warn him a second time. After that, have nothing to do with him. You may be sure that such a man is warped and sinful; he is self-condemned (Titus 3:9-11).

The leader who is skilled in dealing with conflict has an obvious interest in its origin. There are at least five interrelated factors in the **origin of an intrapersonal conflict**, and they are as follows:

(1) Unresolved developmental conflicts which may spring from repressed or suppressed pain, and/or an unrealistic and inadequate value system which is manifested in either an overdeveloped or an under-developed conscience.

(2) Recent unresolved conflicts. There are several determinants in the length of time and degree of pain one will experience in working through conflicts. Three are as follows: the number of conflicts the individual is experiencing, when they occur, and whether they are being repressed or suppressed.

(3) Confusing what one felt about what happened to him or her in the past with what actually did happen, as well as the motives of those involved.

(4) Confusing customs, traditions, and personal preferences with objectivity. For example, conflict may be the result of one person confusing customs, traditions, or personal preferences with what the Bible actually says.

(5) Confusing what one wanted to hear (because of conflictual desires or unresolved intrapersonal conflicts) with what was actually said.

The leader who is skilled in dealing with conflict has an interest not only in the origin of intrapersonal conflict, but also in the **origin of interpersonal conflict**. Interpersonal conflict can arise as a result of projected intrapersonal conflicts. Through the defense mechanism of projection, group members attribute their own faults or shortcomings to others. All people have difficulty at times seeing themselves as others see them. Individuals have the tendency to emphasize their own strong points and overlook their own shortcomings. Group members often tend to see in others those characteristics which they cannot accept about themselves. Interpersonal conflict may come about as a result of unhealthy views toward it. Five common views which Christians (especially leaders) have about conflict are as follows:

(1) Believing that conflict in and of itself is sinful. A person may think that he and/or the other individual are sinning if there is a conflict between them.

(2) Believing that group members should be able to work together without conflict. This view often leads to the defense mechanism of denial and projection. Denial often comes through not accepting one's feelings.

(3) Thinking that conflicts manifest themselves only in certain ways. Some group members, including leaders, do not see a conflict in a relationship unless there is an open fight.

(4) Thinking they are dealing with conflict through diverting attention to something or someone else.

(5) Thinking **time heals everything**. Leaders or group members may verbally acknowledge that they have a conflict, but may avoid dealing with it directly. They may consciously or un-

consciously hope that **time** will solve the conflict. They may acknowledge it, but avoid it by never clearly and definitely deciding to confront it.

Although there is a time for everything (Ecclesiastes 3:1) and time is required for problems to be solved, questions to be answered, and healing to take place, time in and of itself does not solve problems, answer questions, and heal wounds. Time itself does not create intrapersonal and interpersonal problems and cannot in and of itself solve such problems. If time solved problems, then man would be only a robot and not responsible for himself and what he does. If time heals everything, then all one needs to do is just sit back and wait for time to do the healing. It is true that through the financial, educational, vocational, marital, and family changes which people experience, they may look at particular problems differently than they did at an earlier time in their lives. But it is not true that time alone brought about this change.

Individuals inappropriately use time to ignore, avoid, or deny their problems or to refuse to seek effective solutions to them. Such misuse of time guarantees that their problems will not be solved, and that they will become more complicated and require more wise use of time to solve them at a later date. Therefore, it is important to see that **time is valuable in problem solutions only in the sense of how an individual uses it.** It is true that a person's memory can become dull over a period of time and forgetfulness can even occur, but that which is not solved in time can be made worse through procrastination. It takes time to learn how to deal with conflict within oneself and in one's relationships, but time alone does not resolve conflicts.

Leaders and group members who say they want to leave conflicts to time may be revealing the following:

(1) They actually are shirking responsibility for themselves and to other group members.

(2) They really do not know what to do and are not willing to be honest with themselves and others.

(3) They are not interested enough in helping other group members with their problems to experience the painful process of growing and learning how to be more helpful.

(4) They do not care enough to risk getting involved.

(5) They do not care enough to use some of their time for learning how to be with another in his or her pain. One of the ways of **being cruel to people** is to dismiss their pain and **let time take care of them.**

One of the most effective ways for a group to use time is for the members to experience their feelings in their seasons (Ecclesiastes 3:2-8), regardless of whether the feelings are painful or pleasant. This being true, **timing** becomes very important in every aspect of the members' lives. The leader and group member who learn to use time creatively learn to live creatively.

A conflict is unhealthy if the members **do not process their pain** (fear, anger, embarrassment, guilt, etc.) of growth and conflict resolution. Emotional pain is inherent in growing or resolving conflicts; therefore, a conflict which otherwise should be healthy becomes unhealthy if the pain is not processed.

A conflict is unhealthy if the group members **are not willing to listen to each other**. Even a healthy conflict becomes unhealthy if those who are in conflict with each other are not willing to listen to one another. For example, according to Paul, legitimate and potentially effective meetings can do more harm than good. He said, "In the following directives I have no praise for you, for your meetings do more harm than good" (1 Corinthians 11:17). There are many reasons why Christians meeting together can be harmful to them, one of which is refusing to listen to one another. Jeremiah stated:

> *This is what the Lord says: "Stand at the crossroads and look; ask for the ancient paths, ask where the good way is, and walk in it, and you will find rest for your soul. But you said, 'We will not walk in it.' I appointed watchmen over you and said, 'Listen to the sound of the trumpet!' But you said, 'We will not listen' " (Jeremiah 6:16,17).*

A conflict is unhealthy if some of the group members **attempt to deal with it outside the relationship** in which the conflict **originated.** This is a principle which leaders find very frightening; therefore, few percentagewise believe it or comply with it. However, the Scriptures are very clear regarding this principle.

The most effective way to deal with conflict is when it first emerges while the group is still assembled. Jesus acknowledged this procedure when He said, "**Settle matters quickly with your adversary** who is taking you to court. **Do it while you are still with him**..." (Matthew 5:25; emphasis mine, JAJ). Jesus points out further that a conflict grows, not dissolves, after individuals leave each other. Instead of a person **forgetting it** (the conflict), according to Jesus, "He may hand you over to the judge, and the judge may hand you over to the officer, and you may be thrown into prison. I tell you the truth, you will not get out until you have paid the last penny" (Matthew 5:25,26). The accuracy of this affirmation is painfully experienced in divorces and church splits.

The urgency of resolving conflicts when they emerge is seen in an earlier exhortation of Jesus. Notice how emphatic He is. "Therefore, if you are offering your gift at the altar and there remember that your brother has something against you, **leave your gift** there in front of the altar. **First go and be reconciled to your brother**; then come and offer your gift" (Matthew 5:23,24; emphasis mine, JAJ).

According to Jesus, an individual may be more spiritual resolving a particular conflict with his brother than attending a specific religious service (offering his gift). In fact, Jesus said that a person should leave a religious service in order to resolve a conflict with his brother. After resolution has taken place, he can more effectively offer his gift.

Jesus again addresses the matter of resolving conflicts within the relationship in which they occur when He says, "If your brother sins against you, go and show him his fault, just between the two of you. If he listens to you, you have won your brother over" (Matthew 18:15).

In conflict resolution and personal growth, it is important that an individual establish that another person, in reality, sinned against him. It is easy sometimes for a Christian to get his feelings hurt (feel rejected and unloved by the other) because of the following interrelated reasons which are not sins:

(1) He was not the preferred and only one in the eyes of the other.

(2) He did not receive frequent and undivided attention from the other.

(3) He did not get his way regarding a personal preference.

(4) Another did not agree with his personal opinion about such matters as marriage, child-rearing, church socials, etc.

If indeed another individual did sin against a particular person, Jesus said he should deal with that matter privately—"**just between the two of you.**" Again, Jesus is emphasizing the fact that conflict resolution is most effective when it is dealt with in the relationship in which it originated. The most appropriate time is **while it is emerging and before the group disbands**.

Jesus recognizes that conflict originates within individuals and between them. However, there are times when a person only becomes aware of interpersonal conflict after the group has disbanded. Even when this happens, Jesus points out that the conflict should be dealt with in the specific relationship in which it originated. Go back to that specific brother or the group in which the conflict emerged. Do not go outside the group or behind another's back to accuse and ridicule.

It is also significant to notice that even when a person has been sinned against, he should **not attack, accuse** (tell him what his motives were—which he cannot do anyway—1 Corinthians 2:11), or **ridicule** the other person. In fact, Jesus makes it very clear that the one sinned against should **show** the other his fault. Jesus is implying that the sin is rather obvious. The motive for approaching the other is to settle the conflict and win him over. However, Jesus recognizes that it is possible for the one doing the sinning not to listen. Then, and **only then,** should others become aware of the sin. It should be understood that the others, the sinner, and the one sinned against are to meet together. When subgrouping takes place within the group, conflicts are **fueled and not resolved**. Anything which happens in the group should be dealt with in the group. If subgroups develop (even if a leader is involved in subgrouping), conflict will only grow and become more out of control. Jesus recognized this, and so taught in principle.

When conflict between two individuals is not resolved, then it is appropriate to include one or two others, but only if subgrouping is not allowed and if there is agreement between the parties to focus on the **sin** and not the personalities involved. The one who sinned and the one sinned against should be in agreement on who the other one or two persons should be.

If the conflict cannot be resolved in the small group, it should be taken to the larger group, the church (Matthew 18:16,17). Very little conflict percentagewise will ever need to be brought before the whole church if Christians follow the instructions of Jesus regarding conflict resolution.

A conflict is unhealthy if the group members **do not resolve their conflict or learn how to manage it.** Solomon talks about this in principle in the following passages:

> *A foolish son is his father's ruin, and a quarrelsome wife is like a constant dripping (Proverbs 19:13).*
>
> *Better to live on a corner of the roof than share a house with a quarrelsome wife (Proverbs 21:9).*
>
> *Better to live in a desert than with a quarrelsome and ill-tempered wife (Proverbs 21:19).*

Obviously, the point is conflict can be damaging and therefore needs to be resolved. Even healthy conflict, if not managed properly, can become unhealthy.

A conflict is unhealthy if the group members refuse to **take responsibility for themselves in resolving it**. Sometimes it is easy for the group to sit back and wait for someone else to take responsibility for resolving the conflict. The fact is, each member of the group should assume personal responsibility for resolving or effectively managing intrapersonal and interpersonal conflict.

Some Conflicts Are Healthy

Conflict is healthy under the following conditions:

(1) It results from the group members attempting to relate to each other.

(2) It results from the group members attempting to move from one developmental stage to another. The group is not going to remain the same throughout its life. Thus, when the group begins developing, there will of necessity be conflict within it.

(3) It results from growth in general. Any group that is growing and changing is going to experience conflict. Therefore, conflict which results from growth is not unhealthy but certainly indicates that the group is healthy.

(4) Even unhealthy conflict becomes healthy if the members process it and constructively learn from it. Solomon said, "I applied my heart to what I observed and learned a lesson from what I saw" (Proverbs 24:32).

Nine Interrelated Reasons Why Some Conflicts May Never Be Resolved

(1) The group members do not truly want them resolved. A person may want the conflict resolved, but may be unwilling to go through the painful process to resolve it. Jeremiah stated, "The prophets prophesy lies, the priests rule by their own authority, and my people love it this way. But what will you do in the end?" (Jeremiah 5:31). He also stated, "This is what the Lord says: 'Stand at the crossroads and look; ask for the ancient paths, ask where the good way is, and walk in it, and you will find rest for your souls.' But you said, 'We will not walk in it.' I appointed watchmen over you and said, 'Listen to the sound of the trumpet!' But you said, 'We will not listen' " (Jeremiah 6:16,17).

(2) The group members do not learn how to work through a conflict. Although there are principles which people can learn and use in conflict management, there are times when they are simply **lost** and do not know what to do. Learning to acknowledge that they are lost and to accept it, not fight it, is important. Otherwise, a person becomes more confused. Isaiah said, "Woe to those who call evil good and good evil, who put darkness for light and light for darkness, who put bitter for sweet and sweet for bitter" (Isaiah 5:20).

Being lost and not knowing what to do is biblical and natural for a group at times. Jeremiah said, "I know, O Lord, that a man's life is not his own; it is not for man to direct his steps" (Jeremiah 10:23).

(3) The group members do not give proper and adequate attention to a conflict when it begins. Most conflict is relatively easy to resolve or manage in its inception. Like a fire, though, it can soon become unmanageable.

(4) The group members fail to have a clear, realistic, precisely defined, and adequate contract and/or to comply with its terms.

(5) The group members do not differentiate the three basic dimensions of a conflict (see p. 19).

(6) The group members do not discover which is the core dimension and focus on it while giving simultaneous and balanced attention to the other two dimensions.

(7) The group members do not understand that conflict means a **contest or fight**, and therefore the issues in a conflict are **alive and powerful.**

(8) The group members do not understand that there cannot be an intrapersonal and interpersonal conflict without emotions being involved. Even the objective dimension of conflict is intrapersonally and interpersonally related. Thus, **a conflict cannot be resolved without dealing with the emotions**. Emotions are powerful; therefore, they need to be recognized, understood, accepted, and worked through caringly, honestly, respectfully, responsibly, and at the proper place and time, and with the appropriate person. One of the worst mistakes an individual (including the leader) can make regarding a conflict is to think that by ignoring his emotions, they will go away. Just because individuals are not aware of their emotions does not mean that they do not have any emotions in a particular conflict. It should be understood that emotions are energy. Energy can be transformed, but it cannot be destroyed. When emotions are not allowed to emerge, or when they disappear from the surface, they are not gone; they just appear somewhere else. In this connection, another serious mistake is made by thinking that time heals emotions. Emotions build up over a period of time when ignored or denied. They do not disappear simply with the passing of time.

(9) The group members do not recognize the strengths of each other and know how to build on them. Paul said,

> "Therefore, encourage one another and build each other up, just as in fact you are doing" (1 Thessalonians 5:11).

A skilled group leader seeks to prevent unnecessary conflict from developing in the group. He also understands that there are unhealthy and healthy conflicts, and he differentiates between the two. He has insight into the fact that some conflicts cannot be resolved unless he can help the group lower its defenses and analyze its resistance to conflict resolution.

3

Are Group Norms A Defense Against, Or A Reflection Of Self?

"... your meetings do more harm than good."

(1 Corinthians 11:17)

What Are the Rules?

Every group has norms. They may be clear, precise, realistic, adequate, and effectively articulated; or they may be ambiguous, contradictory, unrealistic, and inadequate. In any case, there will likely be some unconscious but very forceful rules by which the group is governed. The older the group and the more natural it is (such as a family), the more likely the unspoken (of which the members are aware) and the unconscious rules control the group. Likely, every group has rules of which its members, including the leaders, are not aware.

The group norms are very important because they are the regulatory forces which constrain the group members' behavior. They determine what behavior is permissible and what behavior is not acceptable. The group norms control what matters will be discussed and to what extent a matter will be discussed in the group. Group norms can influence a person to be less of himself or more of himself in a group. For example, will group members be allowed to share personal thoughts and feelings about themselves and other members in the group? Group norms can cause a person to be guarded and defensive or open and flexible. So, what are the rules?

The Bible–A Defense Against Growth or a Guide to Self-Discovery and Growth

How the Bible will be used in this group is a pertinent question. David said, "Your word is a lamp to my feet and a light for my path" (Psalm 119:105). He also stated, "I have hidden your word in my heart that I might not sin against you" (Psalm 119:11). James said, "Anyone who listens to the word but does not do what it says is like a man who looks at his face in a mirror and, after looking at himself, goes away and immediately forgets what he looks like" (James 1:23,24).

While the Bible can be the basis for a person's individual and social growth, it can also be used by him as a defense against his growth. Anything which is potentially good for an individual can be potentially harmful for him also. The Bible is no exception; it can be a burden for one or a means to help him lift his burdens. A person may study the Bible to be enlightened by it or to keep himself in darkness. According to Jesus, some people prefer darkness to light; they fear being exposed (John 3:20,21). This can be just as true of a Christian as of a non-Christian.

A person can use the Bible as a defense against his growth. He can read it to prove **he is right** and **others are wrong.** Defending one's position and being defensive are not the same. In fact, there is a marked **difference** between **defending** one's position and **being defensive** about his position. Defending one's position implies a certain level of maturity. It implies an open, honest, sincere search for **truth.** The defender welcomes a critical analysis of his position. He is willing for another, as well as himself, to look at the reasoning process which led him to such a position. He does not confuse looking at his position and/or being critical of it with looking at him as a person and saying that he is faulty or wrong.

One who is defensive about his position feels threatened and must be guarded and closed as he refuses to look at the reasoning process used to arrive at his position. He may become arrogant and attempt to humiliate the one who is calling his position in question. He most likely has confused his position with himself as a person.

Truth is inherent in God, not man. An individual may search for truth, learn it, and be freed by it, or use it as a further defense against being free. If the Bible is right, it is right because it is God's revelation. Therefore, an individual is right to the extent that he does what God says, in the way and for the reason that He says it. When a person gets caught up in his confusion and arrogance, though, he may actually try to use the Bible to prove he is right and others are wrong. It is as though **he is truth** instead of his reading the Bible to discover truth.

The Bible can be no more than a **mere proof-text** to an individual. A person may read it just to find statements that he thinks support his view. When this is the case, it is used as a defense mechanism.

The Bible can be the core of a person's health and wholeness to the degree that he understands and assimilates its principles consistently and adequately. On the other hand, the Bible misunderstood and used as a defense mechanism against one's personal growth can be hurtful and unhealthy.

Performance of Acts (Rituals) Can Be a Vehicle Into or Away From Self

Religious acts or rituals may be a way to avoid finding and expressing oneself, or they may be a means of self-expression. An individual needs to be related to himself, God, and others; and one of the purposes of religious acts is to enable a person to become related. One of the subtle dangers of religious acts, though, is that a person can do the **right act** for the **wrong reason**. A particular act may be an expression of what is in one's heart, or it can be a mere pretense. **What one does does not necessarily reflect what one is**. These suggestions are clearly set forth in the Scriptures. Jesus said, "You hypocrites! Isaiah was right when he prophesied about you: 'These people honor me with their lips, but their hearts are far from me. They worship me in vain; their teachings are but rules made by man.' " (Matthew 15:7-9; see also Isaiah 29:13).

It is true, "A happy heart makes the face cheerful, but heartache crushes the spirit" (Proverbs 15:13). Likewise, "Even in laughter the heart may ache, and joy may end in grief" (Proverbs 14:13). Solomon said, "Better to be a nobody and yet have a servant than pretend to be a somebody and have no food" (Proverbs 12:9). He also said, "One man pretends to be rich, yet has nothing; another pretends to be poor, yet has great wealth" (Proverbs 13:7). Jesus stated, "Watch out for false prophets. They come to you in sheep's clothing, but inwardly they are ferocious wolves" (Matthew 7:15).

Religious expression which is healthy and helpful must come from clear and unmixed motives. As has been set forth, one can use religion to pretend, avoid, and deny certain parts of himself. He can ask the right kind of questions not for the purpose of learning, but for the purpose of attempting to test or trick another. This is illustrated in the parable of the good Samaritan.

> *On one occasion an expert in the law stood up to test Jesus. "Teacher," he asked, "what must I do to inherit eternal life?"*
>
> *"What is written in the Law?" he replied. "How do you read it?"*

He answered: " 'Love the Lord your God with all your heart, with all your soul, with all your strength and with all your mind'; and, 'Love your neighbor as yourself.' "

"You have answered correctly," Jesus replied. "Do this and you will live."

But he wanted to justify himself, so he asked Jesus, "And who is my neighbor?" (Luke 10:25-29).

Avenues of Worship–Defense Mechanisms or Means of Self-Revelation, Self-Expression and Self-Growth

There are essentially five avenues through which an individual can worship God. They are communion, study and proclamation of the Word, prayer, singing, and financial contribution. These avenues can be means of self-discovery and self-expression, or they can be simply meaningless rituals or repetitive acts which lead to boredom and isolation from oneself, others, and God. They can lead to health and wholeness or to sickness and disintegration of self and relationships. The Bible is very clear that a person can have a form of godliness but deny its power (2 Timothy 3:5). A person can look good on the outside but be rotten on the inside—clean on the outside but dirty inside (Matthew 23:25-28)—laughing on the outside but grieving on the inside (Proverbs 14:13).

What Are Defense Mechanisms and Why Are They Necessary?

In order for one to understand what defense mechanisms are and why they are necessary, an individual needs some understanding of personality theory. Freud's view of personality is perhaps the clearest in helping one understand what defense mechanisms are and why a person utilizes them. He conceptualized personality in three levels: the id, the ego, and the superego. In Freudian theory, the **id** represents the instinctual urges and drives within a person. It is that level of personality which contains human motives and drives. The **ego**, according to Freud, is the rational, reality-oriented level of human personality which develops as the child becomes aware of what the environment makes possible and impossible for him. Freud saw the **superego** as the level of personality which contains the moral or ethical aspects—the **conscience** of a person.

The id consists of instinctive urges and develops first. The ego and superego develop later. The id and superego are in conflict with each other and, in normal personality development, the ego acts as a buffer between the two.

Freud theorized that the id impulses do not pass away or are not abated by the passage of time if they are not satisfied as a person develops. Thus, the individual who does not find satisfactory ways of dealing with these basic drives, tendencies, or impulses has a continual buildup of tension. In order to cope with this tension, the ego therefore instigates a defense reaction which may take a variety of forms termed **defense mechanisms**. There are three significant characteristics of defense mechanisms, and they are as follows:

(1) Any and all defense mechanisms are **reactions to anxiety** (or tension) which may be healthy or unhealthy. Defense mechanisms, then, are implemented by a person to protect himself from perceived harm—physical and/or emotional. A major problem with defense mechanisms occurs when they are unhealthy and control a person instead of his controlling them. A problem also exists when defenses are unconsciously or automatically raised and a person neither understands the reason for them nor is able to lower them at his choosing. Although defense mechanisms are necessary to health and happiness, a person needs to grow to the point that he can accept himself and his situation and can analyze and process his defenses to the point that he can lower or raise them at his will. Any behavior which results in a reduction of anxiety while not leading to an excessive maladaptive distortion of reality can be considered healthy. In a person's growth process, he needs relationships in which he feels accepted, respected, and cared for as a person. Such relationships must enable the person to be open, honest, and responsible and to **feel safe** enough to lower his defenses in order to analyze and work through the **controlling components** of them.

(2) Defense mechanisms are **distortions of reality**. Since anxiety results from clashes between the id and reality, or between actual behavior and conscience (superego), it follows that a person may try to reduce his anxiety by attempting to change reality. These attempted changes in reality by a person involve distortion. The nature of defense mechanisms is to protect oneself, but it should be understood that not all reactions to threats to self-esteem are reality-oriented. Sometimes a person distorts reality in ways designed not to change the situation, but simply to make himself look better (to himself and others) and feel safer.

(3) Defense mechanisms are **unconscious**. It should be understood that a person does not deliberately and consciously distort reality in order to reduce his anxiety. The ego of a person, which is dedicated to self-protection, instigates these reactions without the conscious volition of the individual.

Common Defense Mechanisms Which a Person Uses to Protect Himself

(1) **Rationalization**. Jesus recognized and referred to this defense mechanism when He said, concerning those who had been invited to the great banquet:

> *"But they all alike began to make excuses. The first said, 'I have just bought a field, and I must go and see it. Please excuse me.' Another said, 'I have just bought five yoke of oxen, and I'm on my way to try them out. Please excuse me.' Still another said, 'I just got married, so I can't come' " (Luke 14:18-20).*

When a person rationalizes, he finds logical but false reasons for past, present, or future behavior. His reasons protect him from recognizing and admitting his own weaknesses and shortcomings. To recognize and admit his real reason would hurt his self-esteem; therefore, he rationalizes or excuses himself. A person should realize that he is not aware of using defense mechanisms. If he were aware of rationalizing, rationalization would offer no defense to protect him.

(2) **Intellectualization** is related to rationalization because it is an attempt to verbalize as a means of avoiding one's feelings—in particular, one's anxiety. An anxious person, for example, may very well be a talkative person. However, the person doing the speaking, as well as the individuals listening, may not be aware that the verbalizing is a means of avoiding one's anxiety. Intellectualization is frequently used in Bible classes and religious discussion groups as a means of avoiding the anxiety which the group is feeling or would feel if they began to become self-reflective. Often in religious groups, the Bible and intellectualization are used in conjunction with each other as a defense mechanism. In other words, the individuals may frequently apply the Scriptures they are studying to other people, or they may be concerned only with the academics of that passage or passages they are theoretically considering. They may look only at the etymological meaning of the words, at the grammatical construction, or at how often a word is used in other places. This method of study certainly has a place, but when it is used consistently and without application to the individuals in the group and what is going on with them, it is most likely a defense mechanism.

(3) **Repression.** Whenever a person has feelings which make him extremely anxious—particularly those which conflict with what he has learned to be **right**—these feelings may become repressed. Sexual and aggressive feelings, for example, can cause anxiety, particularly when a person has been severely punished (verbally or nonverbally) as a child for being aggressive or for showing sexual curiosity. Most individuals learn to deal with such feelings in a mature way, and consequently these feelings do not evoke anxiety. In some cases,

however, these feelings are repressed. Repression is not like suppression; repression is an unconscious act—the individual is not aware that it occurs. (Suppression occurs when one consciously tries to avoid thinking about certain things.) It should be remembered, though, that repressed feelings are not simply forgotten. Even though a person may not be aware of such feelings, they still affect the individual's behavior.

(4) **Denial**. A person who has forgotten a traumatic experience, whether by suppression or repression, is not aware of feeling anxiety. Therefore, **denial** is an easy defense mechanism for a person to utilize. Denial is related to repression or suppression because that of which a person is unaware can easily and sincerely be denied. Denial is one of the common defense mechanisms used by individuals in religion. It is relatively easy for religious individuals to deny their anxiety and their personal, marital, family, and group problems. They often sound boastful about not being afraid and will argue with anyone who would dare question them about being afraid. This happens because they attempt to cope with their anxiety by denying it; if one is not aware of his anxiety, it is easy for him to deny it sincerely.

(5) **Compensation**. When a person feels inferior in certain aspects of his behavior, he often tries to compensate. For example, a poor student may defend against his feelings of inferiority by excelling in other areas. Feeling inferior about one aspect of behavior does not necessarily lead to excelling or attempting to excel in another. A poor student may work extremely hard to become a good student. Sometimes a person goes to extremes in other areas to make up for his inferior feelings in a given area. When this happens, it is called **overcompensation**.

(6) **Projection**. Through this defense mechanism, an individual attributes his faults or shortcomings to others. Therefore, through projection, a person comes to believe that his own undesirable feelings or inclinations are really more descriptive of others than himself. Projection is the defense mechanism which a teacher or minister may use when teaching or preaching about sexual matters. When a person

goes into detail about the **motives** of other individuals, he may very well be describing his own feelings. For example, he may be like the Pharisee of whom Jesus spoke: "The Pharisee stood up and prayed about himself: 'God, I thank you that I'm not like all other men—robbers, evildoers, adulterers— or even like this tax collector. I fast twice a week and give a tenth of all my income' " (Luke 18:11,12). The point is that **individuals are more alike than they are unalike**, but no one can really read the mind of another and **know his motives**. In fact, Paul raised this very question when he asked, "For who among men knows the thoughts of a man except the man's spirit within him?" (1 Corinthians 2:11). One problem with projection is that the person who uses it tends to think he is a **mind reader**. Sometimes a sparse knowledge of psychology contributes to his deception.

Projection leads to fault-finding and shifting the blame to others instead of taking responsibility for oneself. Projection is an attempt to shield oneself from his pain of self-criticism and reproach. Naturally it is easier to rebuke others or to damn inanimate objects than to accept the source of conflict and pain in oneself. Of course, there are times when others are at fault.

An individual who has intense prejudice, intolerance, criticism, and cynicism likely uses projection as an attempt to protect himself. Such a person is prone to see in others his own unexplored tendencies. An individual who is overly concerned about the morals of others is no doubt fighting some of his own projected inclinations. For example, he may have certain natural desires which have remained unfulfilled. Seeing others fulfilling the same desires which he has unconsciously desired to fulfill may generate excessive anger toward those individuals as well as intolerance of them. Thus, it becomes easy for that person to thank God that he is not like others. Projection, then, is rarely, if ever, constructive.

(7) **Sublimation or Displacement** is the method a person uses to direct his instincts, desires, and tendencies in ways which are acceptable to himself as well as others. Sublimation, then, is a process of diverting one's instincts, desires, and tendencies

from socially unacceptable expressions or those which may have threatening consequences to expressions which are more acceptable or safer. To illustrate, when a person thinks it is not safe to express his hostility against a particular individual, he may find himself **kicking his dog** or playing a competitive sport. An individual experiencing sexual feelings may masturbate instead of expressing them in sexual intercourse. Sublimation may be used consciously or unconsciously.

(8) **Segregation or Compartmentalization** is a defense mechanism which an individual develops to avoid his conflicts and contradictions. The individual does not see the interrelatedness of his thoughts and actions. It is difficult for him to see the contradictions between his **worship on Sunday** and his **living on Monday**. It is impossible for a person using this defense mechanism to become integrated.

The Value of a Contract

One of the first things which a skilled leader does is to obtain a contract with the group. A contract is simply an agreement between the leader and each member of the group. In focusing on the three dimensions of conflict, it becomes very important for the leader to include each group member. The contract should deal with what, when, where, and how the members (including the leader) will relate to each other. The leader and the group need a **clear, precisely defined, realistic, and adequate contract**.

A contract will help the leader and each group member to have a specific understanding of how they are to relate to each other. Otherwise, the leader and/or the individual group members would go into the relationship with preconceived ideas about their tasks and how they are to respond to each other. These assumptions may be diametrically opposed and unrealistic and thus cause a **clash**, which is conflict. In fact, much conflict grows out of misunderstandings and is due in part to ambiguous generalization and infrequent communication. Perhaps the most valuable use of time in the beginning of a group is to lay the ground rules clearly and adequately for the way every person is going to relate—what **rights and responsibilities each person has**.

If a leader is going to be effective in helping a group strengthen itself through focusing on the three dimensions of its conflict, there needs to be an agreement on the following components of the contract. Each member (and especially the leader) must not only agree to these rules, but must be deeply committed to a fair, consistent, and persistent implementation of them.

(1) All group members agree that the contract clearly differentiates each member's responsibilities.

(2) All members agree that they have a right to have their feelings, to express verbally and nonverbally what they feel toward other members, to listen and respond to the feelings other members are or are not sharing, and to process or work through their own feelings as they are emerging or as soon thereafter as would be appropriate.

(3) All members agree on how, when, and where they will relate.

(4) They agree on what is acceptable and unacceptable to share in the group.

(5) They agree on clear, realistic, and adequate rules which will govern how, when, and where they will attempt to resolve conflict in the group, since conflict will be inevitable.

A contract will help the group members to know in advance that the leader anticipates that conflict will develop in the group at some time. Thus, when it comes, it is not a shock or surprise. Furthermore, the leader and the group members have worked out their fundamental rules in advance, and know something about what to do when conflict does emerge. This does not mean that the group member can and will follow the rules. One of the leader's responsibilities is to help train the group members not only in developing an effective contract, but also in following the rules once the contract is agreed upon. Thus, the group members gradually learn how to be more effective in managing their own conflicts.

A contract increases the group members' sense of security and therefore lowers their anxiety because they know what is expected of themselves and the other members. Hence a clear, realistic, precisely defined, and adequate contract helps **prevent unnecessary, unhealthy, and unrealistic conflict** and becomes the **structure** in which conflict can be resolved or more effectively managed when it emerges.

4

There Cannot Be Conflict Without Emotions.

"He looked around at them in anger and deeply distressed at their stubborn hearts..."

(Mark 3:5)

What One Feels About Feelings Makes It Easier or More Difficult to Accept Feelings

Individuals in a group have feelings regardless of whether or not they are aware of them. They have such feelings as acceptance, disgust, fear, anger, expectations, pride, joy, and sadness. The leader, as well as the group members, may have **feelings about his feelings.** These feelings about feelings may cause individuals more difficulty than the feelings themselves. If a leader and the group members are going to "encourage one another and build each other up" (1 Thessalonians 5:11), they need to accept each other's feelings and learn how to process or work through them. Thus, it becomes very important (if members are going to be strengthened) that they (especially the leader) understand that a person in his developmental process may have learned the following:

(1) To be **ashamed** of his emotions, especially his need to give and receive genuine affection, both verbally and nonverbally.

(2) To be **afraid** of his emotions. He fears his own angry, affectionate, or sexual feelings. He may be afraid because in the past he expressed them disrespectfully and irresponsibly. He may be afraid because he thinks if he allows himself to feel them, he will be overwhelmed and will act inappropriately and irresponsibly.

(3) To feel **guilty** when his emotions emerge. His guilt may come from believing that to feel or think something is as bad as doing it. It may come from believing **he should not** have certain feelings; therefore, if he does, he is sinning. His guilt may come from **acting out** in the past, and he does not want to deal with those painful feelings. It may come from believing that to **talk out** a feeling is the same as **acting it out**. In the past, a person may have **talked about** a feeling and then **acted it out**, and because of the experience, he may have confused the two (Jones, **Counseling Principles for Christian Leaders**, pp. 122, 123; see also pp. 125-128).

Feelings Are Friends, Not Enemies

Contrary to what many individuals think, feelings are not to be viewed as though they were a malignancy. It is true that some feelings are enjoyable and some are painful, but none are unhealthy. In fact, a person is healthier if he learns to accept and experience all of his emotions, preferably while they emerge. However, there are times and circumstances when an individual cannot process his feelings as they emerge.

Instead of viewing feelings as dangerous to oneself and therefore to be avoided, a person should see them as necessary to one's health. Solomon said, "An anxious heart weighs a man down, but a kind word cheers him up" (Proverbs 12:25). He again stated, "Hope deferred makes the heart sick, but a longing fulfilled is a tree of life" (Proverbs 13:12). He also said, "A heart at peace gives life to the body, but envy rots the bones" (Proverbs 14:30).

Anxiety is often viewed as being unhealthy but, in reality, it says to one that he or a value he holds feels threatened. Therefore, it should signal a person to be alert, to analyze his anxiety to determine the specific fears, and then to confront those fears. When this is done, a person feels better, not only because he has processed his anxiety, but also because he has accomplished something worthwhile to himself.

Frustration is a feeling seen by some individuals as an enemy. When one looks at it more discerningly, though, he can see that frustration is what one feels when he is not accomplishing his desired goals. An individual may be setting unrealistic and unachievable goals; nevertheless, frustration is a natural feeling which one should experience when he is not achieving what he desires.

Disappointment hurts! The degree of pain in disappointment is contingent upon the significance of the loss to a person. Thus, disappointment is a natural feeling which one should experience when **his idols fall** or when an event which is important and for which he had planned does not take place.

Jealousy is what a person feels when he is not receiving love in the manner and on the level he needs. When one is feeling **jealous**, he feels insecure. A person feels insecure because he is low on love. Love is synonymous with security. If a person understands the meaning of jealousy, he is then aware that either he needs more love or he needs it to be expressed in a different way. However, if a person focuses on his jealousy and not on his need for love, he will become more jealous. Nevertheless, jealousy is a person's friend because it simply says to one that he is low on love and therefore feels insecure. There is a marked difference between a feeling of jealousy and being a jealous person. (Jones, **I Never Thought It Would Be This Way**, pp. 60-64, 105.)

Embarrassment is a person's friend because it is what he should experience when he exposes himself or is exposed by others without being intellectually, emotionally, and physically ready to be exposed. It is God's way for a person to protect himself from undesirable exposure. A person needs to learn that no one can experience his embarrassment but himself. He may feel the whole world sees his magnified nakedness with the same clarity and precision as he does. Embarrassment can be seen as one's friend, then, if he learns that he is not ready for the exposure he feels. Thus, this feeling becomes a protection for an individual rather than his enemy. For example, it should be a signal for one to be quiet instead of continuing to talk or overreact (Jones, **I Never Thought It Would Be This Way**, pp. 69, 70).

Understanding One's Heart

The biblical concept of **heart** includes man's intellectual, rational, volitional, and emotional activity (Lusk, pp. 58-75). There is also a technical difference between emotions and feelings, although the two are used interchangeably in this book. Gaylin said:

> **Emotion** *is the general term which encompasses the feeling tone, the biophysiological state, and even the chemical changes we are beginning to understand underlie the sensations we experience;* **affect**, *introduced from psychoanalysis, is used to describe the dominant emotional tone of an individual, and is particularly used in relationship to our recognition of the feelings of others;* **feeling** *is our subjective awareness of our own emotional state. It is that which we experience; that which we know about our current emotional condition* (Gaylin, p. 1, emphasis mine JAJ).

In order for an individual group member to manage any feeling effectively, he must have a basic understanding of his emotions. He must be able to accept and experience his emotions freely, openly, and responsibly at the proper time and in a suitable place with the appropriate person (Jones, **I Never Thought It Would Be This Way**, pp. 27-49).

God made human beings, and they are valuable because of the nature God gave them. The emotions are an inherent component of a person's nature. Since the Bible does not say that one innate component of a person's fundamental nature is more valuable than another part, it is correct to conclude that each part of a person's basic nature is of equal value with the others. Therefore, the emotions are as valuable as any other part of one's personal nature.

Since a part of people's nature is the heart (emotions) and they are expected to serve God with the heart (Luke 10:25-28; Matthew 15:8; Ephesians 5:19; and Colossians 3:23), it becomes very important for people to learn how to experience their emotions while simultaneously serving God through various means. Since a part of the person is the heart and the heart is the seat of the emotions, it follows that a person has certain innate rights to emotions.

All Group Members Have the Right to Have Their Feelings as Well as to Experience Them

The word **right** carries the idea that a thing is in order, suitable, and fits a person's nature. If emotions are inherent in human nature, then feeling or experiencing emotions suits that nature. Therefore, when individuals feel or experience emotions, they are not doing something against their nature, but are acting in harmony with it. If people are born with emotions (which are God-given) and if they have different emotions (which they do), then they have a right to feel or experience all of their emotions. If God created individuals with the emotions of anger, jealousy, anxiety, or fear, they have a right to experience them.

Perhaps most group members, including the leader, would say that a particular member has a right to some feelings but not to others. This may be stated implicitly more than explicitly. The Bible nowhere teaches this idea because it would be contradictory to human nature. Emotions are so interwoven that to experience one feeling necessitates the ability to experience the opposite. In other words, the degree to which individuals can experience joy is in proportion to the depth which they can experience sadness. It should be understood that some emotions hurt and some are pleasant, but all are good for a person to experience (Gaylin, 1979).

Job, David, Jesus, and Paul are four individuals in the Bible who experienced their pleasant as well as their so-called negative emotions. I use the word **so-called** because such emotions which are frequently referred to as negative (sadness, fear, anger, jealousy, etc.) are not necessarily negative. Emotions are energy, and energy is force. Force needs to be channeled in the right direction at the **appropriate time**, in the **proper place**, in **adequate amounts,** and toward the **correct person or situation**, or else it can be harmful to an individual.

Emotions were given to human beings to experience—not to deny or project. Obviously, individuals should not experience their positive feelings to the exclusion of their negative ones or vice versa. People who do this frequently and for long periods of time harm their emotional, physical, and spiritual health. Individuals need to experience or feel their emotions while they are emerging in relationships. Many group problems (a family is a group) are rooted in the fact that the group members often feel ashamed, afraid, or guilty if they feel their emotions.

All Group Members Have the Right to Feel the Feelings They Have Toward Other Group Members

This fact is true whether the feeling is pleasant or unpleasant, and whether the person is a leader or one of the group members. Individuals have the right to feel whatever feeling they find themselves experiencing toward another. Therefore, in the eyes of God, they need not be ashamed, afraid, or guilty. Jesus felt both anger and compassion toward others (Mark 1:41, 3:5, 8:2; Matthew 9:36, 14:14, 15:32). To my knowledge, neither Jesus nor Paul ever apologized for having feelings toward someone regardless of what those feelings were.

All Group Members Have the Right to Express Their Feelings Verbally and Nonverbally

If the group members are going to "encourage one another and build each other up" (1 Thessalonians 5:11), they must exercise this right. Expression of feelings should be done openly, honestly, specifically, caringly, respectfully, and responsibly. Each of the preceding words becomes very significant in the effective management and resolution of group conflict. This is not to say that people should never raise their voices or otherwise manifest their feelings through the eyes, facial expressions, speech rate, gestures, and posture. It is to say that the body does reflect one's emotions, and individuals should intentionally use the body in communication. Solomon said, "As water reflects a face, so a man's heart reflects the man" (Proverbs 27:19). Feelings should also be expressed at the **appropriate time**, in the **proper place**, in **adequate amounts**, and toward the **appropriate person** while they are emerging in the relationship. Solomon stated, "There is a time for everything, and a season for every activity under heaven" (Ecclesiastes 3:1). Job, David, and Jesus certainly expressed their feelings. The following exemplify this fact.

> *If only my anguish could be weighed and all my misery be placed on the scales! It would surely outweigh the sand of the seas—no wonder my words have been impetuous (Job 6:2,3).*

> *Be merciful to me, Lord, for I am faint; O Lord, heal me, for my bones are in agony...I am worn out from groaning; all night long I flood my bed with weeping and drench my couch with tears (Psalm 6:2,6).*

My guilt has overwhelmed me like a burden too heavy to bear. My wounds fester and are loathsome because of my sinful folly. I am bowed down and brought very low; all day long I go about mourning. My back is filled with searing pain; there is no health in my body. I am feeble and utterly crushed; I groan in anguish of heart...My friends and companions avoid me because of my wounds; my neighbors stay far away...For I am about to fall, and my pain is ever with me. I confess my iniquity; I am troubled by my sin...O Lord, do not forsake me; be not far from me, O my God. Come quickly to help me, O Lord my Savior (Psalm 38:4-8,11,17,18,21,22).

For troubles without number surround me; my sins have overtaken me, and I cannot see. They are more than the hairs of my head, and my heart fails within me (Psalm 40:12).

Why are you downcast, O my soul? Why so disturbed within me? Put your hope in God, for I will yet praise him, my Savior and my God. My soul is downcast within me; therefore I will remember you...I say to God my Rock, "Why have you forgotten me? Why must I go about mourning, oppressed by the enemy?" Why so disturbed within me? (Psalm 42:5,6,9,11).

My soul is overwhelmed with sorrow to the point of death. Stay here and keep watch with me (Matthew 26:38).

My God, my God, Why have you forsaken me? (Psalm 22:1; Matthew 27:46).

Contrast the **feeling words** in the above passages with the **accusations, condemnations, and ridicule** often expressed by individuals. **How, when, and where** a person expresses feelings is very significant in effective communication and conflict management. **How** refers to expressing one's feelings genuinely, warmly, caringly, respectfully, intentionally, firmly, softly or loudly, and responsibly. **When** refers to the time element. The most effective time for one to expose feelings is while they are emerging in a given relationship. Also, a person expresses feelings to another when that individual is ready emotionally, intellectually, and physically. It is necessary to allow adequate time in order to listen to and deal with what is shared by an individual. It should be kept in mind, though, that some sharing is hard to do and very difficult to accept (John 6:60). Jesus called attention to the fact that a person may not be able to receive all that an individual can say. He said, "I have much more to say to you, more than you can now bear" (John 16:12). **Where**, of course, refers to the place, which needs to be private and suitable for effective communication or conflict management.

All Group Members Have the Right to Listen and Respond to the Feelings the Other Group Members Are or Are Not Sharing

Individuals not only have a right to listen to other group members' feelings as they are shared, but they also have a **responsibility** to listen (Jones, **I Never Thought It Would Be This Way**, pp. 41-50). A practice of the Golden Rule requires this of any individual (Matthew 7:12). Listening and responding to feelings requires considerable training; therefore, the leader may need to spend time learning, as well as teaching the group members this art. Although listening and responding to feelings are skills to be learned, it is relatively easy for young children to learn them. However, most adults find the art of listening and responding to feelings difficult to learn because they have to be re-educated to learn it. Obviously, this learning process means they will have to change. **Change is painful and is met with resistance.** In an ongoing relationship, **that which is resisted is that which will persist**. Thus, it becomes very important for a leader to analyze the resistance and help the group work through whatever is causing it.

Listening is absolutely necessary in order to resolve or effectively manage group conflict. It can be accurately said that some people talk too much, but likely no one ever listens too much. Obviously, listening means different things to different individuals at different times. One who truly listens to another communicates the following messages:

(1) I care about you.

(2) You are important and valuable as a person.

(3) You are not **bad** and **terrible** although you share your **painful feelings** with me.

An effective listener is one who **values listening**. Jesus said, "For where your treasure is, there your heart will be also" (Matthew 6:21). Since the art of listening may not be greatly valued by the group members, the leader may have to do some teaching in this area. The leader should be aware and teach both explicitly and through modeling that one of the most powerful ways to build another person's self-esteem is through **genuinely listening** to that individual. An effective listener listens to **understand**—not to answer, attack, condemn, or humiliate the speaker (Jones, **I Never Thought It Would Be This Way**, pp. 57-81). God told Ezekiel, "Son of man, listen carefully and take to heart all the words I speak to you" (Ezekiel 3:10). Jesus stated, "Consider carefully what you hear" (Mark 4:24). He also stated, "Therefore consider carefully how you listen. Whoever has will be given more; whoever does not have, even what he thinks he has will be taken from him" (Luke 8:18).

A group member's resistance to listening in an open, accepting, and non-attacking manner to another (especially if the group member is angry at the speaker, or for whatever reasons feels he has been hurt by him) is in proportion to his having recognized, accepted, and worked through his fear, guilt, and shame in the area in which the speaker is struggling. This is one reason why feelings need to be processed as they are emerging or as soon thereafter as possible. Thus, one listens to the **same pain** (in principle) in oneself while also listening to the speaker share his or her pain.

An effective listener **listens** and **responds** to the other person's **feelings**. Solomon said:

> *A gentle answer turns away wrath but a harsh word stirs up anger...the tongue that brings healing is a tree of life, but a deceitful tongue crushes the spirit (Proverbs 15:1,4).*
>
> *If a ruler's anger rises against you, do not leave your post; calmness can lay great errors to rest (Ecclesiastes 10:4).*

A man finds joy in giving an apt reply—and how good is a timely word! (Proverbs 15:23).

The heart of the righteous weighs its answers, but the mouth of the wicked gushes evil (Proverbs 15:28).

A wise man's heart guides his mouth, and his lips promote instruction. Pleasant words are a honeycomb, sweet to the soul and healing to the bones (Proverbs 16:23,24).

He who answers before listening—that is his folly and his shame (Proverbs 18:13).

An effective listener listens to do **analogue reasoning**. Is what is being communicated analogous to some other experience? Paul did analogue reasoning when he was in Athens (Acts 17:22 following). Jesus often listened to people and responded in this manner. He frequently used similes.

An effective listener is **physically, mentally, and emotionally rested and ready to listen**. An effective listener has planned to have enough time and has arranged for an appropriate place.

Effective listeners listen **with the total person**. They try to **see** with the **eyes, hear** with the **ears**, and **understand** with the **heart**. When this is accomplished, change can take place within both the speaker and the listener. Interpersonal problems can be solved only when the individuals involved are willing to change. But they cannot really change until they can see with their eyes, hear with their ears, and understand with their hearts (Isaiah 6:9,10; Matthew 13:17).

What, how, and **how much** a person **hears** at a particular time are contingent upon such factors as the following:

(1) How tired the listener is physically, mentally, and emotionally. It should be understood that everyone has his limitations. No one can be all things to all people all the time.

(2) The listener's degree of shame, fear, and guilt about what is being shared. The further these feelings reach into a person's past experience, the more difficult it will be to hear what another person is sharing.

(3) What the listener was trained to hear while growing up, as well as the degree of appropriate training since physical maturity. Was the listener trained to listen just to words and not to feelings? Was the listener trained to hear **all** a person says before responding? Did the listener learn to hear a few words and then interrupt—telling the other person what is wrong with that view, etc., or changing the subject completely?

(4) What the listener thinks is important. People do not really listen to what is **not important to them**. The group members may have been erroneously trained to think that **feelings are not important**, and therefore they **do not listen and respond** to the **speaker's feelings.**

It is a fact that individuals hear what they want to hear, although they may be unaware of it (Titus 1:15; Acts 17:11; Jeremiah 5:31; Matthew 13:15). It is also true that persons hear what they are afraid they will hear. An individual's anxiety greatly influences what is heard in communication. The one-talent man illustrates this point (Matthew 25:24-30).

(5) The amount of time a listener has. A person cannot really listen when in a hurry; therefore, it becomes important to arrange for ample time in which to communicate. It takes time to dismiss other things from one's mind and to get ready to hear someone else. To ignore these factors is to reduce one's listening effectiveness.

(6) The appropriateness of the place. Selecting a place is important to effective listening. It should be private, away from distracting noises and abrupt and unnecessary interruptions.

All Group Members Have the Right to Process or Work Through Their Feelings

The Bible is very clear about a person processing his feelings. It precisely states that an individual should experience or release his feelings. It does not state anywhere that a person should **keep any of his feelings bottled up inside himself**. In fact, Solomon said there is "a time to weep and a time to laugh" (Ecclesiastes 3:4). Paul said, "Rejoice with those who rejoice; mourn with those who mourn'' (Romans 12:15). He also said, ''In your anger do not sin: Do not let the sun go down while you are still angry...Get rid of all bitterness, rage and anger, brawling and slander, along with every form of malice'' (Ephesians 4:26,31).

It is clear from the above passages that one's feelings, whether pleasant or unpleasant, are to be shared (processed), not bottled up within one's body. Processing and working through feelings are two ways of talking about the same thing. The following interrelated steps are involved in processing feelings:

(1) A person must become **aware** of having particular feelings.
(2) An individual must **correctly identify** his feelings.
(3) A person must **understand** and **accept** the origin of his feelings.
(4) An individual must **analyze** his feelings and their origin thoroughly.
(5) He needs to **express** the appropriate amount of feelings at an appropriate time, in the appropriate place, toward the correct person(s) or event.
(6) In working through feelings, a person must experience them—not just say feeling words; for example, crying until one is finished.

It is sometimes suggested that individuals do not have a right to their feelings because it is not right to be hateful or envious or jealous. It should be clear that if individuals understand their emotions and learn how to process or work through them, they will not experience being hateful, envious, and jealous persons. Hatred is the result of individuals not processing their irritations when they emerge or shortly thereafter. Individuals who are filled with hatred have a right to this feeling, but having a right to it does not mean they have a right to keep it and allow it to increase. They should have gotten rid of it a long time ago. So while they have a right to their hatred, they have a right and a responsibility to get rid of it appropriately.

A person who experiences anger, envy, or jealousy has other feelings which need to be worked through. While one needs to identify the anger, envy, or jealousy, successfully working through these feelings necessitates that a person recognize, accept, and work through the feelings which **underlie** the feelings of hatred, envy, or jealousy.

There are feelings which cause the feeling of anger. There are feelings which cause envy and jealousy. Identifying these feelings and working through them while simultaneously identifying anger, jealousy, and envy is the effective way to deal with these feelings. Denying and avoiding the underlying feelings is an excellent way to intensify one's anger, envy, or jealousy (Jones, **Counseling Principles for Christian Leaders**, pp. 96-102).

Anger is a powerful feeling. A feeling is energy. Energy can be transformed, but it cannot be destroyed. When it disappears from one part of a system, it appears elsewhere in the system. For example, as one object becomes cooler, an adjacent object becomes warmer. Thus, it becomes very important to process or work through one's anger. One of the worst things which can be done is to teach individuals to deny, avoid, or suppress their anger, or to project it onto others. Disguised and displaced anger is much more difficult to deal with than anger which is recognized and sufficiently dealt with while it is emerging.

Individuals do not like to deal with anger because they are afraid of it, feel separated from each other by it, and think that if it is acknowledged and worked through, it would bring further isolation and alienation. This, of course, is not true. When anger is openly acknowledged and dealt with respectfully and responsibly, the feelings of isolation go away as the anger is processed; then warm, **positive** feelings emerge. If correctly labeled, accepted, and respectfully and responsibly expressed, anger can be the energy force which enables a person to take constructive action. This is especially true when an individual is experiencing a reactive depression (depression which results from a loss).

It is also important to understand that anger is a **secondary** emotion. In order for it to be satisfactorily worked through on a continuing basis, not only must it be identified and correctly labeled, but those feelings which cause it must be identified, correctly labeled, and processed likewise. Two emotions which cause anger are jealousy and anxiety. Anger is also caused by a feeling of having been treated unfairly, by unrealistic expectations of self and others, by impatience and, often, by an unrealistic value system.

If anger in and of itself is sinful, then Jesus sinned. Mark 3:5 reads, "He looked around at them in anger and, deeply distressed at their stubborn hearts, said to the man, 'Stretch out your hand.' " It is clear that anger is not a sin. On the other hand, anger needs to be worked through or processed. Paul is very specific about this matter. Notice!

> *In your anger do not sin: Do not let the sun go down while you are still angry, and do not give the devil a foothold...Get rid of all bitterness, rage and anger, brawling and slander, along with every form of malice (Ephesians 4:26,27,31).*

There are three harmful ways to respond to feelings:

(1) Block them out so that one is not aware of them.

(2) Focus on one feeling to the exclusion of other feelings.

(3) Focus on feelings to the exclusion of other reality. To illustrate, individuals need to cry and feel sadness at the loss of a loved one, but a part of reality means that they also need to continue paying the bills, get back to work, and become involved in life again.

One difficulty for group members and some leaders is to take the necessary time to allow the individuals to process their emotions. Obviously, if there is an accumulation of emotions from past experiences which are intrapersonal and interpersonal, processing will take much longer than if the current emotion is only stimulated by something relating directly to the present. One of the mistakes made by group members and some leaders is that they ignore emotions, thinking they will go away, instead of experiencing their emotions—both pleasant and unpleasant ones.

Individuals and their relationships are dynamic. Therefore, feelings are never processed once and for all time to come. Individuals continually need to process them. Feelings need to be momentarily processed and worked through frequently; otherwise, they build up, and take longer and become more difficult to process.

An individual can tell when the feeling has been processed for the time being. Jesus gives an example of this regarding His preparation for death. He spent an hour praying to His Father that, if it be possible, He would let the cup of death be taken from Him (Matthew 26:40). He went away two other times to go through the process again. It could be assumed that on the second and third times, He also spent an hour praying. It is definitely clear that when He had processed His feelings, He was ready to face the inevitable. Notice! He said, "Rise, let us go!'' (Matthew 26:46). In this incident of His life, Jesus demonstrates that individuals are naturally emotionally ready to move on to other aspects of their lives once they have allowed themselves to process or work through their feelings. Leaders or group members who have not had experience in processing their feelings usually get anxious, and attempt to interfere with other group members working through their feelings. This being true, it becomes important to educate leaders and members in how to utilize their five emotional rights in preventing and resolving group conflict.

References

Gaylin, W., **Feelings** (New York: Ballantine Books, 1979).

Jones, J. A., **Counseling Principles for Christian Leaders** (Abilene, Texas: Quality Publications, 1982).

Jones, J. A., **I Never Thought It Would Be This Way** (Abilene, Texas: Quality Publications, 1982).

Lusk, M. W., III, **The Indwelling of Deity** (Atlanta: Private, 1980).

5

What Should We Do With Our Anger?

"In your anger do not sin ... Get rid of all bitterness, rage and anger, brawling and slander, along with every form of malice."

(Ephesians 4:26 & 31)

Leaders and Followers Get Angry

Anger is an experience of every person, regardless of whether he is an infant or elderly, whether he **feels** it or is completely unaware of being angry. Anger is a feeling which is experienced in groups such as a family, congregation, or business. I think anger in religious groups is seldom really recognized, accepted, understood, and processed in a respectful and responsible manner. Therefore, it is a problem to leaders of these groups. I also think anger is one of the underlying causes of personal and interpersonal conflicts, whether in families or churches.

A Leader Needs to Recognize and Label His Anger as Anger–Not Call It Something Else

Most of the people I see neither recognize their anger nor are aware of when they are feeling angry. Many people in the church, as well as out of the church, are not aware of being angry until their angry feelings have built up to the point that they are **mad**. By this, I mean **they do not feel their anger** until it has reached the point where they react in one or more of the following ways:

(1) They have an overwhelming urge to walk out of a business meeting.

(2) They feel compelled to quit attending church services.

(3) They have an overwhelming urge to hit or throw something—perhaps at another person.

(4) They curse someone.

When individuals react as described above, they then talk about being **mad**. This is, in a technical sense, a form of **craziness**. It means they have **lost control of themselves** and usually talk and act very irresponsibly and disrespectfully.

A leader who has a **hot, high, or quick temper** is sitting on a **hot bed of anger** and will usually act irresponsibly or foolishly. That is, he has **stored up anger** and, under frustration or disagreement with another, it is very easy for him to **get mad** or **lose control of himself**. Solomon stated, "A quick-tempered man does foolish things, and a crafty man is hated" (Proverbs 14:17). He also said, "A patient man has great understanding, but a quick-tempered man displays folly" (Proverbs 14:29). He further stated, "A hot-tempered man stirs up dissension, but a patient man calms a quarrel" (Proverbs 15:18). Madow points out that there are two major reasons for quick, open expressions of anger:

> *The individual has accumulated so much anger that only a little more is needed to set him off. This is seen in the person who overreacts to a situation by becoming more angry than is warranted. Such a person has had many dissatisfactions in life and is walking around with a high concentration of stored up anger.*
>
> *The second reason is that the quick-to-anger person has found that anger works and is conditioned to continue its use. If a youngster finds that by having a temper tantrum he gets what he wants, he is encouraged to have another the next time he is denied something. If the next one is equally successful, he will begin to develop a pattern of behavior. Since most people dislike displays of temper, they may cater to the person who behaves in this fashion rather than risk setting off an outburst. The quick-tempered person need not be a very angry one, but rather one who has found that this mode of behavior is effective and is reinforced by further success (p. 36).*

In ongoing interpersonal relationships, the emotion of anger appears in various shapes, quantities, and stages, all of which are called by different names. In this chapter, though, no attempt will be made to distinguish between aggression, hostility, rage, resentment, and anger. There are definite differences between these words, depending on whether the anger is great or small, acute or chronic, new or long-standing, latent or overt. Frequently, anger is expressed in disguised actions as well as words. It is recognized as being anger neither by the person using the disguised words or expressions nor by the **target person** receiving the anger.

There are many words and expressions which a person uses to refer to the feeling of anger. An individual using the words and expressions may not realize that the feeling to which he is referring is actually anger. Any time a person uses words like aggression, resentment, fury, indignation, outrage, wrath, antagonism, crossness, hostility, bitterness, destructiveness, spite, scorn, disdain, enmity, defiance, griped, seething, annoyed, troubled, inflamed, antagonized, exasperated, vexed, furious, provoked, irked, abhor, irritated, hostile, or offensive, he is referring to the emotion called **anger**. Also, when an individual uses an expression such as "He gives me a pain in the neck," "She makes me sick," "I will get even with him," "I am annoyed," "I am irritated," "I am fed up," "You make me laugh," "I am sick and tired of that," or "I am ready to explode," he likewise is referring to the emotion of **anger** (Strecker & Appel, pp. 114,115; Madow, pp. 3-14).

A Leader Needs to Know the Causes of His Anger

It is very important for a leader to learn to recognize and label his anger. It is equally significant for him to understand the **causes** of his anger. In order to be angry and not sin (Ephesians 4:26,27), a leader must learn **to be aware of feeling his anger as well as to express it** (verbally and nonverbally) openly, caringly, respectfully, and responsibly. However, a leader who is just beginning to feel and express his anger will also have a **build-up** of angry feelings from past experiences which will cause him to feel more anger than the current situation or frustration provokes. If he works through his build-up responsibly, he will get to the point where he feels only the anger which is evoked in that particular situation or experience. How long it will take a person to reach this point will vary with every individual. It depends on such factors as the following:

(1) A person's age.

(2) His insight into his anger and its causes, as well as his fear, embarrassment, and guilt at expressing his anger.

(3) The type and frequency of supervision he receives while learning to **share his anger at the appropriate time, in the proper place, in adequate amounts, with the correct person, or in the correct situation.**

A leader should also learn not to dehumanize others when expressing his anger by putting them down verbally and nonverbally, ignoring them, laughing at (not with) them, or refusing to speak to them.

It is **not enough just to feel and express one's anger at the appropriate time, in the proper place, in adequate amounts, to the correct person, or at the correct event—situation.** A leader needs **clear insight** into what is **causing** him to get angry, as well as whether the **causes are realistic.** Most of the anger which people with whom I work have comes from **denying their anger.** Denial causes their anger to build up to rage. Thus, they tend to act impulsively and unwisely. They resign from their leadership roles or stop attending church services. There are other causes for this type of behavior, but denied anger which has built up to rage is often a key factor.

Anger is a **secondary feeling** which may have realistic or unrealistic causes. A person feels anger only after he has had at least one other feeling. That is, anger is generated as a result of an individual's experiencing a primary feeling previous to or simultaneous with the anger (Gordon, pp. 125-129).

This does not mean that a person experiences (consciously feels) his anger or the primary feeling which produces the feeling of anger. It simply states that there are causes (realistic or unrealistic) for a leader or anyone else to get angry. If one is to process his anger effectively, he must **understand and process the feelings which produce his anger.**

The primary feelings which a leader has toward himself and others are what cause him to feel anger. Also, the feelings which one has because an event did not take place or because something happened in a specific situation cause anger. It is a real problem for any person to ascertain what he feels regarding his primary feelings (as compared to what he thinks he **should feel**), as well as to determine within himself if his primary feelings have a realistic cause. Several primary feelings will now be considered to illustrate this point.

Frustration Is a Cause of Anger

A leader will naturally become angry if he is frustrated long enough. However, it is unrealistic for one to think that a Christian should always be easygoing—never get frustrated. A leader who has this view of frustration will tend to deny his anger. He may feel ashamed or afraid or guilty about having anger from being frustrated. Therefore, after a period of time, he will likely experience much more anger than a particular frustrating situation would ordinarily provoke. On the other hand, a person may become frustrated because of unrealistic reasons. For example, he may expect a young child who has never been to Bible study to be quiet and attentive shortly after he begins to attend Bible study. Thus, his unrealistic expectations of the child will cause him to become impatient. His impatience will cause frustration. His frustration will cause him to get angry. But both the anger and the frustration are unrealistically based in this situation.

Unrealistic View of Self and Others Causes Anger

A leader who thinks he **must be perfect** and **everyone** should always **like him** as well as **like what he says and does** is going to experience much more frustration and anger than the person who has a more realistic view of himself and people's feelings toward him and his actions. A leader whose self-esteem is largely dependent on how others feel toward him as well as what they say about him and his actions, will experience frustration and anger frequently because of his unrealistic view of himself and others.

A leader who deeply feels that he **should not be questioned** will experience much more anger than a leader who is open and welcomes questions. It is true that he may neither feel his anger nor be aware of it, but it will **show** in his eyes, neck, face, posture, gestures, or tone of voice when he is questioned. However, his cause for being angry is unrealistic because it is appropriate for followers to question their leaders.

A leader who views himself more highly than he ought (Romans 12:3; 1 Peter 5:3) will not only get angry when his followers question him, but will likely expect them to be complimentary of him and his decisions. If they are not, he will probably become discouraged, frustrated, and angry. Of course, a leader may not recognize his anger as being anger and may not label it as such. For example, he may state that his feelings are hurt. But this is usually a **nice** way of saying he is angry. His anger may be expressed in suggestions about his possible resignation. I have seen several leaders, when questioned or disagreed with by other group members, become angry and suggest that perhaps they should resign. It was obvious that they were angry from their nonverbal communication. Although I have seen this happen several times, I have not seen a religious group respond to a leader's anger appropriately and responsibly. The experience I have had with this situation is that the other group members will either ignore the anger, or become anxious and **beg** a leader not to resign. Sometimes they will get angry and accept his resignation. But when this happens, they do not process their anger, nor does the leader work through his.

A godlike leader's self-concept is that he is **the** authority. His rigidity and need for certainty is in proportion to his feelings of insecurity and uncertainty. He thinks his word should be final. He thinks his children, as well as the members of the congregation (even the brotherhood), should **obey him without question**. Therefore, he will experience much more frustration and anger than a leader who is open, welcomes questions, and freely considers new ideas. He may not be aware of his anger, though. Most of his anger is generated because of his unrealistic view of himself and others.

A leader who humiliates others when he feels anxious will become angry when he is corrected or rebuked. The cause for his anger, though, is unrealistic because it is not respectful to ridicule others, and he should be rebuked. Solomon said, "Do not rebuke a mocker or he will hate you; rebuke a wise man and he will love you" (Proverbs 9:8).

Jealousy Is a Cause of Anger

A leader who has few, if any, really close interpersonal relationships will not have his basic need for love met adequately and consistently. Thus, he will become **jealous and resentful**. He feels jealous because he is not consistently and adequately giving and receiving genuine love on the level and in the manner he needs it. This does not mean that a jealous leader does not try to give and receive love. He likely does **in his own way**. But his way is probably filled with contradictions. A jealous leader usually does not have the trust (in himself and the group members), self-confidence, and patience to risk giving of himself deeply in order that he might receive deep and genuine love. In addition, because he has never received and given authentic love consistently over long periods of time, he does not have insight into how to love, as well as what love really is. A jealous leader tends to relate to individuals whose personal dynamics are similar to his. In so doing, he only reinforces his own jealousy.

When a jealous leader becomes aware that he is having a conflict with the group and the members do not respond to him in the manner in which he thinks they should, he likely begins to have such thoughts as these:

(1) "They do not like me."

(2) "They are unfair to me."

(3) "They are trying to get rid of me."

(4) "They are laughing at me."

These and similar thoughts begin to create the feeling of jealousy, which produces the feeling of anger. Likely, a jealous leader will perceive the group members' behavior or attitudes as proving his suspicions were right. "They really do not love me" or "They are out to hurt me or show me up."

A jealous leader may express his jealousy through certain behaviors or attitudes such as these:

(1) Withdrawing from the relationship or resigning as group leader.

(2) Making cutting, derogatory accusations to group members.

(3) Becoming suspicious (not trusting).

(4) Believing the group members think the worst of him.

A jealous leader is **so low on love** that he thinks he can no longer risk. Therefore, he will not likely confront his suspicions with the group members to check out his thoughts for accuracy. If a jealous leader does share his thoughts and feelings with the group, he will probably do so after he has gotten angry and **out of control**. Instead of sharing them, he will probably **blame, attack, and put down the group members**. Thus, his responding to the group members **will be not** to process the felt conflict, but to **humiliate or overkill** the group members before they have a chance to ridicule him. A jealous leader thinks that the group members are already out to hurt him, and that their treatment of him has been grossly unfair. He assumes **he knows their motives** without asking them. He has not seriously considered an important question which Paul raises: "For who among men knows the thoughts of a man except the man's spirit within him?" (1 Corinthians 2:11).

Even if a jealous leader has an opportunity to establish a relationship with a person who is **real and wants to be genuine** with him, he will not likely cultivate it for the following reasons:

(1) When a felt conflict in the relationship arises, a jealous leader will probably sever the relationship.

(2) He may ignore the felt conflict and the person.

(3) He may refuse to discuss the matter openly, honestly, fairly, and realistically, and to resolve the conflict.

(4) When a conflict emerges, he will likely go outside the relationship in which it emerges and misrepresent the relationship and the conflict to some other person.

The Beechers affirm that:

> *A jealous person is always an angry person. He feels put back in life. While he is in the throes of jealousy, he thinks of himself as impoverished and defrauded. Self-pity strips him of contentment. Both his past and his future seem empty to him. He is conscious only of the gnawing pain of his jealous frustration...The story of self-pity is written on his face (pp. 11,12).*

Although jealousy is an emotion, it is important for a leader to see his jealousy (Beechers, p. 1). Furthermore, it is important for a leader to understand that **unfriendly comparison and unfair competition** are significant components of his jealousy. The Beechers believe that jealousy is the most prevalent symptom of a **Persisting Infantilism,** which means that a person is continuing to act in an infantile or childish manner, in a dependent, leaning, irresponsible fashion (p. 3). **Loss of personal identity** is a constant factor in jealousy (Beechers, p. 39). Paul said, "We do not dare to classify or compare ourselves with some who commend themselves. When they measure themselves by themselves and compare themselves with themselves, they are not wise" (2 Corinthians 10:12). The Beechers state:

> *When a person compares himself habitually with others, he spoils things for himself. He is trapped by his unfriendly comparisons. He can't coexist with his "peacemaker" without feeling put back in his own eyes. Lacking a way to cut him down to size, he builds up tensions that wreck his own health and happiness. In the end, he often prefers to destroy his opposition—as Cain did—as long as he retains his jealous habit of mind it makes no difference whether he has scarcity or abundance—he remains at war with himself and others, as did Cain (pp. 12,13; Genesis 4).*

A jealous leader thinks that everyone he has contact with should always love him (paying little or no attention to others when he is around) and never dislike him. He becomes angry when this is not the case. He gets angry because he feels he should be the **preferred and only one** (Beechers, p. 17). But the maturing person who gives and receives love authentically does not expect any person to like him always. A maturing person understands that jealousy is what he feels when he is not receiving love in the manner and on the level that he needs it. When he feels jealous, he understands that he is feeling insecure because he is low on love. Understanding this, a maturing person focuses on his need to receive more love in different ways. He does not focus on his jealousy (though he acknowledges it) because he knows this will only increase it. A maturing person also recognizes that when he feels jealousy, he feels insecurity, which creates fear. Again, he does not focus on his jealousy, but recognizes that "there is no fear in love. But perfect love drives out fear, because fear has to do with punishment. The man who fears is not made perfect in love" (1 John 4:18).

Paul said:

> *Love is patient, love is kind. It does not envy, it does not boast, it is not proud. It is not rude, it is not self-seeking, it is not easily angered, it keeps no record of wrongs. Love does not delight in evil but rejoices in the truth. It always protects, always trusts, always hopes, always perseveres (1 Corinthians 13:4-7).*

But, a jealous leader is not patient and kind. He is envious, boastful and proud. He tends to be quite rude, self-seeking, and easily angered, and he always keeps a record of wrongs. He delights in evil ("I did not think we could trust him anyway."—"Didn't I tell you!"—"I never did think she would be faithful."), but never rejoices in the truth. (He very seldom, if ever, apologizes to the group or gives compliments, but he is always free with criticism.) A jealous leader seldom protects, never really trusts, has little hope, if any, and frequently gives up—on himself as well as others. In other words, jealousy is the opposite of love.

The Beechers say a maturing individual...

> *...seems to have overcome the habit of jealous competition to a large degree. His source of power or center of gravity lies within himself. He doesn't have to lean or depend on others for his inspiration, support, direction, or approval. He doesn't have to live by the customs and judgments of the crowd. He is sufficiently secure to make his own decisions as to what is right or wrong for him. He remains an inner-directed person in the face of all temptation or babble of voices in the crowd (p. 36).*

Nothing can liberate a jealous leader until he sees that **he is the source of his own pain**. Once he fully understands this, he can invent his own way to deal with his jealousy if he so chooses. But no individual can do anything to help a jealous leader with his jealousy until he is willing to do **anything**—even get rid of his jealousy (Beechers, pp. 39, 6).

Solomon said, "Anger is cruel and fury overwhelming, but who can stand before jealousy?" (Proverbs 27:4). James stated, "For where you have envy and selfish ambition, there you find disorder and every evil practice" (James 3:16). This being the case, leaders should seek to know all they can about jealousy and its related problems, and deal with its prevention and/or correction responsibly.

Impatience Causes Anger

An impatient leader is one who is also easily frustrated and, therefore, one who experiences considerable anger. Essentially, there are two interrelated reasons for a leader being impatient and thus easily frustrated. One is that he has learned his impatience from parents, peers, and other significant individuals. He may have learned it from important others modeling impatience for him. He may have learned that he could temporarily avoid dealing with his frustration if he became impatient and angry. A second reason for a leader being impatient is that he may lack insight into himself, his feelings about a particular situation, and about the person(s) involved in the situation. He also may have certain feelings of which he is unaware.

Processing or working through one's feelings gives a person insight into himself and human nature in general. Those feelings about which an individual still feels shame, fear, or guilt are those which have not been processed. Also, those feelings which a leader is **obsessed** with and **compelled** to act on have not been processed. An individual who processes his feelings learns that "the purposes of a man's heart are deep waters, but a man of understanding draws them out" (Proverbs 20:5). Through the experience of processing one's feelings, a leader learns that there are no easy answers or quick solutions to life's basic problems. Therefore, the more a leader matures and the more understanding of people and their problems he obtains, the more realistic he becomes, the more patience he acquires, and the less anger he experiences.

Several Other Causes of Anger

Mistreatment, unfairness, ridicule, embarrassment, and dishonesty are all causes of anger. It is very convenient for a leader, if he is so inclined, to respond to a group member through one or more of these means. Therefore, a responsible leader who is aware of this possibility is cautious to be fair, honest, and respectful in his relating to the group members. One important factor for a leader to keep in mind, though, is that each one of these reasons very well can be a product of his imagination.

What a Leader Should Do About Anger in Himself

A leader should first recognize that he is angry, and admit it to himself and when appropriate, to the group. Anger of which a leader is aware is much less harmful than unrecognized or unacknowledged anger. A leader may continue to speak of being disappointed, frustrated, or let down, but may be unaware that these expressions may indicate repressed or suppressed anger. Emotions are repressed or suppressed because they are frightening and therefore, are unacceptable to a person. Anger may be denied because a leader feels too embarrassed or guilty about it, or is afraid of it. A leader may be unaware of the conflict between his anger and these emotions.

Anger is an emotional phenomenon, and a leader can deal with it effectively only when he is aware of it as an emotion. Hence, it is not enough for a leader to say intellectually that he is angry. He **must feel his anger** and be able to accept the fact that he is angry (Madow, pp. 107-110).

One of the most difficult steps in a leader's processing his anger is truly recognizing and accepting his anger as anger. Another complex and difficult step is that of **identifying the source of his anger**. If a leader is angry at someone whom he perceives to be powerful and who can therefore harm him in some way, he may look for another subject on which to project his anger. Projection is an unconscious defense mechanism. For example, a leader may be angry at his superior for the way he treats him at work, but may project his anger onto his wife or children at the slightest provocation. He thinks it is safer to direct his anger toward his wife and children than toward his supervisor.

Another reason for a leader's projecting his anger is to avoid embarrassing himself. To illustrate, upon discovering that he has taken a wrong turn in a road, he may blame his wife for distracting him or misguiding him, even though the mistake was really due to his own carelessness. A wife may get furious with her husband if he comments that another woman is attractive, when her anger really comes from feeling that she is not as attractive as the other woman, or that the other woman is otherwise threatening to her.

Guilt can also confuse the real source of anger. A man may be furious with his mother, but because one

> *must not get angry with one's mother, he may find himself exploding at other older women, sometimes wondering himself why he is so angry with them (Madow, p. 111; see also pp. 110-112).*

Once a leader has recognized and accepted his anger and correctly identified its source, he then needs to **understand why he is angry**. Perhaps the most important question for him is whether the reason for anger is realistic. When a leader has anger for unrealistic reasons, he should be aware that there are usually hidden feelings, wishes, or expectations, and they are difficult to face and process. He may need some professional help at this point.

A leader should **deal with his anger realistically**, but this does not mean that a direct expression of his anger is always the best solution. When a leader knows who has made him angry and why, and that his anger has a reasonable cause, a confrontation with the person who provoked his anger may resolve the problem. But this implies expressing one's anger at the **appropriate time**, in the **proper place**, in **adequate amounts**, and toward the **correct person or situation**, preferably **while one's anger emerges**. Furthermore, expression of one's feelings should be done openly, honestly, specifically, caringly, respectfully, and responsibly.

Anger is more difficult for a leader to deal with responsibly when the causes of it are imagined. Then the basic problem is within the leader himself and may require much effort and patience to work through.

A leader should **deal with his anger as soon as it is appropriate for him to do so**. Paul said, "In your anger do not sin: do not let the sun go down while you are still angry" (Ephesians 4:26).

How Should a Leader Respond to Anger in Group Members?

Before a leader can effectively respond to anger in a group member, he must have accepted at least the following:

(1) **Anger** in and of itself is **not sinful**. If anger were sinful, then Jesus sinned because "He looked around at them in anger and, deeply distressed at their stubborn hearts, said to the man, 'Stretch out your hand' " (Mark 3:5).

(2) A group member not only has the right to be angry, he has a **right to be angry at the leaders or other group members**. It is relatively easy for a leader to say he has accepted this, but in an actual situation, he may discover that he has not internalized the concept. A leader who has not accepted that an individual has this right will not be able to respond therapeutically to anger in another person.

An effective step-by-step method of responding to a group member's anger is the following:

(1) Initially, a leader should just listen patiently in order to understand the person who is angry. He should observe with his eyes, hear with his ears, and hopefully understand with his heart (Matthew 13:13-16) the anger that is being expressed, both verbally and nonverbally. An individual who is angry (especially in a rage) does not need for someone to talk to him; he desperately needs an effective listener. He needs someone who will just listen to him as he gets his anger out.

(2) A leader needs to respond calmly and gently to a group member who is expressing his anger. The person who is angry may feel guilty or embarrassed because he is angry. If the group is important to him, he likely feels afraid that he will not be accepted by the group if he expresses his anger. The individual probably feels isolated and lonely and perhaps thinks that expression of his anger in the group would intensify these feelings. Solomon said, "A gentle answer turns away wrath, but a harsh word stirs up anger" (Proverbs 15:1). He also stated, "If a ruler's anger rises against you, do not leave your post; calmness can lay great errors to rest" (Ecclesiastes 10:4).

(3) A leader should help a group member recognize, correctly label, and understand the sources of his anger. He should also teach a member how to express his anger at the appropriate time, in the proper place, in adequate amounts,

and at the correct person or situation, preferably while his anger is emerging.

References

Beecher, M. and W., **The Mark of Cain: An Anatomy of Jealousy** (New York: Harper & Row Publishing Company, 1971).

Gordon, T., **Parent Effectiveness Training** (New York: Peter H. Wyden, Inc., 1970).

Madow, L., **Anger** (New York: Charles Scribner's Sons, 1972).

Strecker and Appel, E. A. and K. E., **Discovering Ourselves** (New York: The MacMillan Co., 1958).

6

The Art Of Listening Is Inherent In The Art Of Leading.

"Consider carefully what you hear."

(Mark 4:24)

"Therefore consider carefully how you listen."

(Luke 8:18)

Listening Is Needed

One of the basic needs of every human being is to have at least one person (preferably more) to whom one can responsibly reveal oneself in a trusting, respectful manner. James and John called this **confession**. "Therefore, confess your sins to each other and pray for each other so that you may be healed. The prayer of a righteous man is powerful and effective" (James 5:16). "If we confess our sins, he is faithful and just and will forgive us our sins and purify us from all unrighteousness" (1 John 1:9). In order for one to confess, there must be one who can and will **truly listen** to the confessor.

A leader may say that he wants to know what the group members are thinking and feeling, but I have observed in numerous meetings that sometimes a leader does not mean this, because **he stops listening** at the point that group members begin to **reveal their heartaches**. He may stop listening when members begin to express those things about which they disagree with the leader. Sometimes a leader will stop listening when the group members confess to the leader those feelings of which the leader himself feels guilty, afraid, or ashamed. For example, one elder once said in a meeting at which I was present that he did not want to know what his class members thought of his teaching or of him personally. At least this man was honest. Many times, the same message is communicated nonverbally. People have said to me in therapy that a particular leader may "say he is interested in me, but when I go and try to talk with him, he gives me the feeling that he is not listening to me and really does not care about me and my problems."

Listening Helps the Group to Prevent and Resolve Conflicts

If a leader knows how to listen and will take the time to listen, he will be able not only to solve problems in the group, but also, to a great extent, to prevent their development. Listening, though, is a skill that is only learned through diligent study and assimilated by continual involvement with people at a deep level of listening.

Every individual has worth, and a leader has the responsibility to help build a group member's sense of self-esteem or self-worth. One of the most effective ways in which this can be done is through listening to a person as he struggles to communicate how he feels and what he thinks about himself, others, and the program of the local church.

Members Are Not Made for Programs– Programs Should Be Made for Members

The above subheading implies the possibility for a basic distortion in a leader's or follower's perception of spirituality—what it is and how it is developed. Likely, no Christian (especially a leader) would agree that **members are made for programs**. However, the confusion, frustration, hostility, and unhealthy conflicts which evolve over **programs** suggest that **some Christians believe that members are made for programs**. Christians should not think they are beyond such misunderstanding, because the Pharisees thought that man was made for the Sabbath (Mark 2:27). Paul said of the Corinthians, "Your meetings do more harm than good" (1 Corinthians 11:17). Jesus said of the Pharisees, "You hypocrites! Isaiah was right when he prophesied about you: 'These people honor me with their lips, but their hearts are far from me. They worship me in vain; their teachings are but rules made by man' " (Matthew 15:7-9; see also Isaiah 29:13). This being the case, the thoughts suggested in the above subheading deserve serious attention and adequate critical study.

James should be taken seriously when he said, "Do not merely listen to the word, and so deceive yourselves. Do what it says" (James 1:22). Doing what the Word says necessitates one's **becoming** what the Word says. However, a person can intellectually and physically comply with certain commands without assimilating them. There is a marked difference between having a balanced and adequate educational curriculum, taught to students on their developmental level in ways which help them assimilate the truths into their character structure, and memorizing a few Scriptures to use defensively to prove that one is right and others are wrong. In addition, an individual may do many things which are Scriptural and morally good without ever understanding the meaning and purpose for doing them. While **doing** is important, it is of little value unless the one who is involved sees how a particular need is being met through such activity. One's activities must do more than meet a particular need on the same level all the time. Since a person has a variety of needs which must be met on different levels, religious activity should be designed to help him meet his various needs at their different levels. Repetitive acts focused on the same needs at the same level soon become meaningless and boring to an individual.

A mistake which an individual may make (and many do) is to use certain religious acts to escape attempting to meet particular needs while trying to meet other needs which cannot be met by those acts. To illustrate, a public confession cannot replace the need for private confession. Taking communion cannot replace the need for brotherly fellowship. Encouraging others to be active religiously cannot replace the need which one has to be responsible in his own family relationships. Seeing the speck in another's eye cannot replace the need to see the plank in one's own eye. Although one need may be more predominant at a given time, every need must be met if an individual is to be whole. One need cannot be met at the sacrifice of another and the person remain healthy. This is easily seen in the physical realm; a balanced diet is needed, but it cannot be substituted for the need for exercise.

The Hebrews writer and Jesus should be taken seriously at this point:

> *Therefore let us leave the elementary teachings about Christ and go on to maturity. Let us not lay again the foundation of repentance from acts that lead to death, and of faith in God, instruction about baptisms, the laying on of hands, the resurrection of the dead, and eternal judgment. And God permitting, we will do so (Hebrews 6:1-3).*

> *Woe to you, teachers of the law and Pharisees, you hypocrites! You give a tenth of your spices—mint, dill and cummin. But you have neglected the more important matters of the law—justice, mercy and faithfulness. You ought to have practiced the latter, without neglecting the former. You blind guides! You strain out a gnat but swallow a camel (Matthew 23:23,24).*

It is my conviction that any church activity should be designed by the leaders to meet the particular needs of those who participate. When developing a program, one of the first considerations should be what particular need or needs this program is being designed to meet. **Leaders need to get away from the false assumption that everybody in the congregation should be involved in everything that is going on in the congregation all the time**. Therefore, in selling a program to the congregation, instead of attempting to make people feel guilty if they do not participate, leaders should approach the introduction of the program from the point of view that it is designed to meet certain intrapersonal and interpersonal needs of those who participate. It should be understood by leaders that a religious activity may have ceased to be rewarding to an individual because of his growth. As a person grows, his activities must change, and he must have his needs met at different or deeper levels or he loses interest in participating in them. When an activity becomes uninteresting and boring to an individual, he needs to evaluate it in terms of his needs, and his analysis should reveal just why it has become meaningless to him. Leaders need to understand that a person has a variety of needs to be met on different levels at different times; therefore, church activities should be designed and altered in their implementation to meet those needs on the level desired.

Leaders need to perceive clearly that Christianity is far more than **church attendance** and **church programs**. Unless they help their followers assimilate truth to depths which allow the truth to govern every aspect of their lives, there will be more Christians who become spiritually sick and die. Furthermore, it should be understood that programs may or may not have anything to do with the essence of Christianity. They may be simply a way for leaders to stroke their egos under the guise of spirituality. If this is the case, spirituality diminishes in both the leadership and the congregation.

Programs should help members develop spiritually, but sometimes leaders leave members feeling that **programs are more important than members**. Programs should be developed for people, but people should not be programmed for church activities. The church can survive without its programs, but not without its members. **Members, not programs**, are the church.

Why Do Leaders Not Listen?

If listening is so important, why is it that sometimes leaders do not listen? This is certainly a complex question, and no general answer would apply equally to every leader in every situation. Yet, there are some basic reasons which any leader should take into consideration, especially when he finds that he is not listening to a particular person or group. The reasons given are not complete, and they are not given in the order of their importance. They all overlap and are interwoven, though one or more may be predominant in a given situation.

A Leader May Not Listen to a Person or Group Because He Feels Afraid, Ashamed, or Guilty about His Own Feelings

Perhaps a leader is **not aware of his feelings**. Nevertheless, verbally and nonverbally, he teaches certain concepts about his feelings. He may teach concepts which are not Scriptural. One false concept which is taught, whether implicitly or explicitly, is that feelings are **bad or sinful** and should be suppressed. When such teaching is believed, matters become more complicated.

In order to really listen to a person, a leader must be willing to accept an individual's feelings. (Acceptance does not involve approval or disapproval.) The leader must also be able to listen to and for the feelings which a person is expressing, usually more nonverbally than verbally. It is an established fact that a person cannot genuinely listen to the feelings of another person if he shares the same feelings and feels shame or guilt about them, or has not recognized, accepted, and worked through them. A sin which a leader will not accept and really listen to in another person may be the same sin (in principle) which he has neither accepted nor forgiven in himself. When a leader hears things from another person or the group which stir up similar things which he has repressed, he is likely not only to stop listening, but to start projecting his own feelings onto a particular individual or the group as a whole. This happens frequently in some Bible classes and business meetings. Furthermore, those things about which a leader feels shame or guilt, or has not recognized, accepted, and processed will become barriers to him in attempting to relate to others and to lead them. Also, he will probably unconsciously read his own feelings into what a particular person is saying and, because he is confused, will lose his objectivity and very likely will become part of the problem or conflict.

There is no experience more likely to call forth a **leader's own inner conflicts** than a meaningful relationship with a troubled person or group. That is why every conscientious leader should practice self-analysis, as well as consider seeking professional assistance to help reveal his own weaknesses, blind spots, and prejudices, and to evaluate his total fitness for his work as a leader.

Every person needs to be liked by others. The more inferior and insecure a leader feels, the less he can withstand the tremendous pressure which results from not being liked by the group at all times. To **avoid his anxiety**, he may simply try to be a **group pleaser** instead of a **group leader**. He may even think if he disappoints the group in any way, he or it will disintegrate. Since the members may need a godlike leader, he may feel that he will disappoint them if he does not come across as omniscient and omnipotent.

Sometimes it is very difficult to be a leader. The pressure which comes from **resistance** and from being disliked may feel overwhelming to a leader. He may think he does not have the strength to undergo the alienation and loneliness which one feels as the direct result of being a leader. Alienation and loneliness may be experienced by a leader as the result of resistance, dislike, and rebellion from the group. He also may experience it as a result of his being at a different point in his growth process from where the members are in theirs.

The pressure to conform to the group's wishes is not new, as exemplified by Aaron's response to the people when they wanted gods who would go before them (Exodus 32:1-6). Aaron responded to the people's wishes and made them a golden calf. An anxious leader may respond to the group's wishes and give them what they want instead of being objective and perhaps helping them to deal with their resistance to getting what they need.

A particular individual may use his leadership role as a defense mechanism against growth instead of as a means through which to grow personally while simultaneously leading others in their growth process. The potential misuse of power by an individual is seen in the qualifications for elders. For example, an overseer "must not be a recent convert, or he may become conceited..." (1 Timothy 3:6). Conceit is not inherent in being a recent convert because it grows out of feelings of insecurity, inferiority, and inadequacy, and not out of feelings of self-esteem, self-control, competence, and maturity. Perhaps a word of caution is in order at this point. The number of years a person has been a Christian does not in itself mean that a particular individual will not become conceited if appointed to the eldership. The underlying issue really has to do with the level of maturity a person has acquired, as well as the meaning power has for him, and not just the length of time he has been in the church.

An accurate indicator of how a leader might use his power in the church would be the way he functions in his family and in other relationships where he has power. Most individuals use their best manners in public and are polite and considerate when guests are present. So, if this is the extent of one's knowledge of how a person functions in his family, it is very limited and may be unrealistic. To illustrate, often ministers, elders, and deacons are in the process of getting a divorce before anyone else in the congregation perceives a problem. Thus, there may be a great deal of ignorance and many false assumptions which cloud an individual's interpretations of how people really are.

The possibility of a person misusing his power is also seen in the qualification "not **lording** it over those entrusted to you, but being examples to the flock" (1 Peter 5:3, emphasis mine JAJ). I discuss appropriate self-disclosure or being a good example in **Counseling Principles for Christian Leaders** (pp. 137-150).

Appropriate modeling becomes more difficult when the group is growing through a developmental crisis and in the initial stage when a leader is seen as a benevolent god. (Hartman and Gibbard, 1974; Bion, 1959; Kaplan and Roman, 1963; Slater, 1966). Appropriate modeling becomes extremely difficult for a leader when the group is going through a reality testing phase. The group goes through several reality testing phases. Perhaps one of the most critical phases is when the group first begins to discover that the leader is not a god and cannot meet all of their needs when and as they want them met.

The second most critical phase is when the group begins to discover that a leader is not omniscient and omnipotent. The group members begin to see the leader's weaknesses, inconsistencies, and contradictions. Thus, the group members may become very critical of their leader and dissatisfied with him. The fight (whether passive or aggressive) is usually in proportion to the leader's need to be seen as omniscient and omnipotent. The more rigid and controlling the leader needs to be, the more intense the struggle between the group and the leader is likely to become. The intensity may be transplanted into passivity or blind obedience, or the group members may become resistant and rebellious.

Testing can force a leader's rigidity and authoritarianism to be more clearly manifested. On the surface, the rigid and authoritarian leader appears to be one who has answered all his questions and solved all his problems. In reality, though, he is not secure in where he is and what he knows. He has used rigidity and authoritarianism as a way to cope with his anxiety because he has not resolved his inner conflicts. This is why he becomes defensive and often hostile when questioned about a particular program, belief, or practice. This also is why he cannot be flexible and accept differing points of view.

A leader cannot realistically help another group member accept the sin he has committed, work through his various feelings, and deal responsibly with the consequences thereof unless the leader is dealing responsibly with his own sins. This is not to suggest that a leader should talk about his sins irresponsibly and inappropriately; it is to say that he must come across as a **caring, respectful**, and **responsible** human being who **also sins**. People have shared with me in therapy that they could not talk with their leaders because the leaders communicated verbally and nonverbally that they really never sinned. Thus, the group members believed that the leader or leaders would not understand and be able to help them with their painful problems. This is not to say that leaders intend to communicate such; nevertheless, the fact remains that individuals do interpret their leaders in this manner.

Suggesting that leaders actually sin could be interpreted to mean that such an acknowledgment would encourage group members to be careless and sinful. Some may even think that the group members would lose respect for their leaders if they knew the leaders had sinned. Certainly, it is never wise to share anything about oneself unless it is appropriate and the situation calls for it. When one chooses to share, only that experience which is pertinent to the particular situation should be shared, and then only provided that the leader is comfortable, and that there is a relationship of trust, concern, respect, and responsibility. It is not wise for a leader to share his sins in a group out of shame, guilt, fear, and compulsion. The **nature** and the **strength** of a relationship are two other factors which help to determine what and how much is shared.

In Paul's day, people had the idea that since grace was abundant, one could live carelessly. They thought that since grace was plentiful, a person could be forgiven regardless of his carelessness. The Scriptures clearly teach that to acknowledge that a Christian sins and that forgiveness is possible does not give one a license to sin (1 John 1:8,10, 2:1,2; Romans 6:1,2).

An effective leader is aware of his sins and especially his struggle with "the sin that so easily entangles" (Hebrews 12:1). It is possible, however, for a leader to be unaware of sins in his life. Those who lead others should not forget that they easily can be deceived or blinded by their own sinfulness. Passage after passage in Holy Scriptures teaches this fact, and group members observe their leader's self-deception and inconsistencies. They may not understand them clearly or articulate them forcefully and convincingly to their leaders. In fact, leaders may be so closed and defensive that the group members will not even attempt to reflect to them their negative reactions, to the leaders as persons as well as to their ineffective communication.

A leader may communicate (even unaware) that he thinks he has **solved** all his problems, **answered** all his questions, **accumulated** all knowledge, and thus is the **dispenser of truth** to the group. Obviously, it would be difficult to ask anyone like this for help. This is especially true of the group who has known the leader long enough to see through this type of facade. Contrary to what leaders might think, the vast majority of individuals can accept sin or mistakes in a leader **provided that he is fair, open, honest, sincere, and apologetic, and that he perseveres**. What hurts a leader with the group is not that the members know his mistakes and his struggles, but rather that he is closed, rigid, authoritarian, opinionated, and conceited while continually attempting to present himself as flawless.

An effective leader presents himself as being in a process of personal growth, too. He approaches **sin** as **dangerous**; he sees its **consequences as painful, inevitable, and necessary to deal with responsibly and thoroughly**. At the same time, he is very **sensitive** to a particular group member's **shame and guilt**, and communicates (especially nonverbally) that he **accepts** the group member and will **not condemn** him. A leader may say he can do this, but group members have shared with me through the years that they felt **condemned to hell**, and that **it appeared that their leaders did not care what would happen to them**.

A Leader May Not Listen to Feelings Because He Thinks They Are Not Important

An individual will not listen to what is not important to him. There is a tendency in the Lord's family to deny or ignore feelings. Some think that if a leader does deal in any way with feelings, people will automatically turn to emotionalism and sins of various kinds. In my therapy practice, I have found that emotionalism and sinning with one's emotions are the direct result of individuals failing to accept their feelings and not expressing them openly, honestly, specifically, caringly, respectfully, and responsibly. Man is so made that if he does not learn to accept and appropriately express his feelings, they will eventually express themselves in ways that are inappropriate and irresponsible. For example, the following are some extreme forms of expressing anger: rape, incest, murder, and physical and emotional abuse of others.

A Leader May Not Listen Because He Does Not Want to Get Involved with Another Person

Real listening demands that the listener turn off the television, lay aside the newspaper, and pay enough attention to the person to learn what he feels and how he thinks. This takes time because the presenting problem is usually not the underlying problem. A person usually goes through a period of testing before he expresses what he really feels or thinks. An individual may really not be aware that he is testing the listener. Furthermore, a person may not be aware of the underlying problem when he begins talking; but as he talks, he may become aware of it. Real listening also means the listener cares enough about the troubled person that his involvement will be seen as concern for the hurting group member. Paul expressed it this way: "Rejoice with those who rejoice; mourn with those who mourn" (Romans 12:15).

Teaching (whether formal or informal) is one method of involvement with people. **Teaching** is also one form of leading, and it certainly **discloses a leader's vulnerability**. **A leader may be afraid of involvement because he is afraid of being vulnerable**.

A presentation is a true exposure of the teacher. Although faulty interpretation by the group member is possible, as a person is teaching, he is revealing the type of individual he is. A group member cannot get a comprehensive view of the leader from one lecture, but the presentation does expose a leader as he is during that hour.

When a member criticizes or compliments a leader's teaching, he is in a very real sense criticizing or complimenting the leader. The question of whether or not the compliment or criticism is justified does not change the fact that through the presentation, a leader reveals himself—his weaknesses (ignorance, prejudices, inconsistencies, defenses, etc.) as well as his strengths.

Every leader has certain vulnerabilities about which he does not want everyone to know. Everyone is probably unaware of some of their vulnerable areas, and it is possible that a leader may want neither himself nor others to see what these weaknesses are. Inasmuch as teaching exposes one for possible attack, it is wise for a leader to know his weaknesses and not try to hide them. Although it is difficult and painful to know oneself, a leader should seek to recognize, accept, and verbalize, when appropriate, his vulnerabilities, wherein lies his real power.

When anyone attacks a person's vulnerable areas, there is pain and resistance, and probably resentment and discouragement. A leader who becomes deeply discouraged is one who has been consciously or unconsciously hiding from his vulnerabilities. Although a leader can hide from himself (see James 1:22,26; Romans 12:3; 1 John 1:8) and, for a while, from others, he needs to recognize that he cannot hide from those whom he teaches and leads in other ways for weeks, months, and years. It is difficult enough for a leader to confront an area of vulnerability in himself of which he is aware and which he accepts. If a leader is not aware of a vulnerable area and does not want to look at it and accept it, he most likely will become frustrated, angry, and discouraged. He perhaps will stop leading if there is much criticism. If a leader does not resign, he may simply get into a fight with the members and become involved in a power struggle rather than a creative growth process.

A leader should understand that members who criticize a certain weakness or inconsistency in a leader frequently do not perceive deeply and clearly how vulnerable a leader is in a given area. They are not aware of how damaging these criticisms can be to his self-esteem. In fact, the group members may not even be aware that a leader is vulnerable at the point where confrontation or criticism is made. What they may be responding to (perhaps without being aware of it) are the leader's ambiguous expressions and ambivalent feelings which he is consciously or unconsciously trying to deny or hide.

A leader may try to cover up his faulty knowledge, poor preparation, and weaknesses by presenting a particular lesson with a rigid, arrogant, and defensive attitude. When members begin to make critical comments or to question him, he may feel threatened and become even more defensive, rigid, and arrogant. He may verbally attack the members, trying to embarrass them for even thinking, much less making critical comments or asking questions. Often this sets off a competitive attitude of trying to prove each other wrong. What can be even more damaging in this power struggle is when the leader and the group move away from the subject or question under consideration and spend their time in disguised ways of attacking each other in the name of Bible study. Eventually, one side may think it has won, but the victory is hollow. The group members may stop coming to class. They may begin to argue, nag, complain, or become distractive in various other ways. A leader may get so confused and frustrated that he quits trying to teach a particular class. In the meantime, many unchristian seeds have been sown. Among these corrupted seeds are unsolved frustration, anger and distrust (usually disguised), and rigid, defensive attitudes.

A leader who is rigid, defensive, and arrogant is trying to cover up (consciously or unconsciously) something within himself which he does not want to accept because it causes him to feel disgust, fear, shame, or guilt. He is afraid to look honestly and realistically at himself. The anxiety this attitude produces is tremendous, and it becomes more difficult to cope with the longer the leader tries to teach. It becomes so frightening and depressing that a leader may give up and quit or just fight back. When this is the case, neither he nor the group members process their frustration, guilt, anger, depression, and anxiety. How much better it would have been if only they had been honest with themselves, accepted their weaknesses, and dealt realistically with them.

One of the sins frequently committed in some Bible classes is that of a leader and the group members pretending with each other that they are not weak at certain points. (This usually takes place on a preconscious level.) Thus, they avoid looking at their weaknesses, accepting them, learning how to strengthen them, and growing more mature. One way of avoidance is spending the class time talking about how weak and sinful others are.

Alexander Campbell was correct in affirming that the Bible "speaks of man as he was, and also as he will hereafter be; but it dwells on man **as he is, and as he ought to be...morally and religiously" (The Chris-**

tian System, p. 3). Although the twenty-one Epistles in the New Testament were written to Christians to instruct them in how to live, one would get the impression from some Bible classes that they were written exclusively to people in the world.

Paul had his thorn in the flesh (2 Corinthians 12:7) and weaknesses (2 Corinthians 12:10), and each child of God has an entangling sin (Hebrews 12:1). It is neither a sin nor something of which to be ashamed to admit that a Christian (even a leader) is weak at certain points. One's strength comes when he knows, accepts, and effectively utilizes his weaknesses. This is the way he can use them constructively. A person's weaknesses control him when he does not know what they are and is afraid to find out. When an individual tries to hide his weaknesses from himself, he antagonizes interpersonal relationships. Also, unknown and unaccepted vulnerable areas in a person will actually control the individual to the point of unhappiness and even self-destruction. Paul said, "For when I am weak, then I am strong" (2 Corinthians 12:10). One's power and security as a leader lies not in being egotistical, rude, defensive, and rigid, but in recognizing, accepting, and verbalizing, when appropriate, his vulnerabilities. This permits a leader to communicate (verbally and nonverbally) that he is flexible, open, warm, understanding, and considerate. Such communication motivates (directly and indirectly, consciously and unconsciously) the group members to reciprocate; this helps to create an in-depth learning situation.

One valuable lesson a leader can teach the group members is that he accepts them where they are in their growth process. He can help them feel free to question him on any point they wish. He can demonstrate openness and honesty without embarrassing them.

A leader needs to understand that communication takes place on a verbal and nonverbal level—the nonverbal level being the most significant. A leader's tone of voice, facial expressions, body posture and movement, gestures, speech rate, et cetera, communicate to a greater degree and on a deeper level than his words.

The nonverbal communication can contradict or complement the leader's verbal expressions. It does not matter what a leader says if his nonverbal communication is sending a contradictory message. The group member may respond to the verbal message, but the nonverbal communication will have the most influence on them.

Emotional growth is painful, but this type of pain is therapeutic. When a person suppresses or represses his weaknesses and sins and does not accept and work through them responsibly, he is asking for chronic pain. It may be in the form of depression and anxiety, which is frequently expressed in a rigid, defensive, and hostile manner.

A leader who is realistically sensitive to his vulnerabilities can be genuinely sensitive to the vulnerabilities of the group members. Such awareness and acceptance can enable both the leader and the group members to grow intellectually, emotionally, and spiritually. Mature growth requires development in all three of these areas.

A Leader May Not Listen Because He Is Too Preoccupied with His Own Problems, Too Involved in Other Matters, or Too Tired

It takes time to listen. If a leader is too preoccupied with his own problems or other matters, too busy, or too tired, he cannot genuinely listen. If this is the case, he will not really listen to the person who has come to him. However, the leader should give the individual a brief explanation as to why he cannot listen at that time and then immediately set up another time when the two can meet.

It may be difficult for a leader to openly acknowledge his preoccupation with his own problems, his involvement in other matters, or his being too tired to listen. It is a fact that Christian leaders and their followers do get tired, and sometimes they grow weary (regardless of whether they acknowledge or accept it) of attending worship services and various related activities. Leaders and their followers also get tired of growing personally, of being married, and of rearing children. They may feel ashamed, afraid, or guilty because they get tired.

Paul said that Christians do get weary, and exhorted the Galatians to become aware of this fact. He stated, "Let us not become weary in doing good, for at the proper time we will reap a harvest if we do not give up" (Galatians 6:9). Although being fatigued is a part of being **weary**, the word **weary** carries with it the idea of **losing heart and becoming discouraged. A Christian can be tired and at the same time be very much encouraged**. Thus, it is important for leaders in the church to make clear distinction in their own minds, as well as to aid others in doing so. Hence, leaders should become more enlightened in the dynamics of being tired and weary—they should see **being tired as natural and normal and being weary as a danger signal.**

It is a fact that people become tired of doing good, but it does not help for leaders to ignore the fact, pretend it does not happen, avoid it, or preach sermons and teach lessons that cause the members to feel guilty for getting tired. Perhaps it would be wise for leaders to look at what causes people, even themselves, to get tired. Four reasons why individuals get tired are as follows:

(1) A person gets tired at times working on his personal growth, marriage, family, and church responsibilities for the same reason he gets tired physically. Church leaders seem to have no problem accepting that it is normal for people to tire physically. For example, no one seems to have a problem with an athlete's getting tired. However, some of the same people think it strange, abnormal, and weird for a person to tire emotionally and spiritually. Therefore, if a person perceives getting tired as being weird, abnormal, and sinful, he will likely become weary.

If it is sinful to be tired, and if a person is tired, it is easy for him to become discouraged or lose heart because he feels there is no hope for him. Since there is no way a Christian can grow without getting tired, there is likewise no hope for him because, if being tired is sinful, he continuously sins.

(2) A person gets tired because of boredom or monotony. To illustrate, the individual who engages in the following practices will probably get tired and very likely will become weary, especially when faced with various life crises:

(a) Using the same words in the same order in every prayer.
(b) Saying the same expressions (with the absence of affect or exaggerated and phony affect); for example, being slurpy sweet or super nice to his spouse, children, or group members.
(c) Experiencing the same bland order of worship services or Bible classes.
(d) Going through the same thoughtless ritual while teaching, preaching, or visiting others.

(3) A person may get tired because he has outgrown the level of teaching or participation which he is experiencing in a congregation. The writer of Hebrews speaks of this issue when he says, "Therefore let us leave the elementary teachings about Christ and go on to maturity" (Hebrews 6:1). Careful thought and planning should be given to analyzing the age levels, needs, and interests of a particular congregation. Once this is done, a curriculum should be critically planned and developed for that specific congregation.

Individuals have shared with me through the years that their Bible classes and the sermons they heard were primarily centered around the Gospels and Acts and first principles. It is true that people at certain points need very simple and elementary doctrinal lessons, but it is equally true that all of the people do not need that level of instruction all of the time. To illustrate, individuals come to me sharing that they are having problems with themselves, their marriages, and their families. They also say they seldom hear sermons or have classes which deal in a realistic and helpful manner with their problems. Others have shared that the sermons they hear and the classes they attend are so elementary that they are not helpful.

Leaders need to be aware that if they are providing only first principle-type lessons for persons who have been in the church for thirty years, then they have some spiritually malnourished individuals who are already in the process of becoming weary; a percentage of them are going to end up leaving the church. Furthermore, leaders need to understand that if all they are providing is a **constant diet of new approaches and fads** in attempting to deal with the problems of conversion, restoration, and personal, marital, and congregational growth, they and their followers are not only going to become tired, but a certain percentage are going to grow weary. Two basic reasons for such are as follows:

(a) Fads are useless in terms of sound educational principles.

(b) People will soon burn out on any approach and become weary if it does not do the following:

(1)Meet the specific needs of the group members.

(2)Deal with the particular interests of the group members.

(3) Answer their fundamental questions.

(4) Help the group members to solve basic problems which they are having within themselves (intellectually, spiritually, and emotionally), in their marriages, in their families, and in their congregations. This is not to suggest in any sense that new approaches should not be developed and that variety should not be used in sermons and Bible classes. Variety is necessary to prevent burn-out, as well as to aid individuals in their growth process.

(4) A person may become tired because he has been given or has assumed responsibilities for which he is no longer suited, in which he is no longer interested, or which no longer meet his needs on the level he needs at a given time. Obviously, leaders need to know themselves and the group members.

In the process of his development, a person may assume many responsibilities which suit his needs and interests at certain stages of his development. If he continues to grow, though, his interests and needs will change. Thus, there needs to be modification in his responsibilities. For example, one who has become an elder may at one time have been a janitor, Bible teacher, song leader, or preacher. As an elder, though, hopefully he has matured to the point where he can develop people to assume his former responsibilities. This frees him to be able to carry out his current responsibilities at a much deeper level and with more maturity.

It is a given fact that any person gets tired more quickly performing tasks which he sees as unconnected than an individual does who sees the interconnections of his various responsibilities. An integrated person has several functions, but does not feel split or divided. Thus, he does not see himself as being pulled in different directions when assuming different responsibilities.

Leaders need to understand that growth necessitates change, and change means a number of things, such as the following:

(a) The members assume new responsibilities.
(b) They modify or give up old responsibilities.
(c) The members need to function at a deeper level in those responsibilities which they keep.

Rather than encouraging the members to develop in such a manner, some leaders become jealous and angry when members are no longer doing their specific assignments the way they once carried them out. Leaders may even try to convince the group members that they are not as religious as they once were.

Inasmuch as individuals do get tired and getting tired is not a sin, it seems that one could assume that resting at times and for the right reasons is not sinful, but healthy. Jesus rested at times (Mark 6:31,32; Matthew 8:24). Thus, it seems that it would be Scriptural and appropriate to teach individuals not only that they need to rest, but also how to rest. I certainly do not propose to know all the methods, but the following are some ways in which an individual may discover how to rest. Although they are simply stated, this does not suggest that they may be easily and quickly assimilated by an individual.

(1) A person may experience a great deal of release from stress upon discovering that it is appropriate for a Christian both to be tired and also to rest.

(2) An individual may experience stress release in discovering and utilizing his freedom. A leader may have assumed considerable pressure by thinking that he can be responsible **for** the group members. A leader can be responsible **to** and **with** the group, but he cannot be responsible **for** them; the more he tries, the more stress he will experience. The less a group leader or member needs to please or impress others, and the more he does what he does by choice and not by compulsion, out of growth and not out of guilt and fear, the less stress he will feel.

(3) A leader or group member may experience stress release in learning and accepting that he does not know how and is not able to do everything. There is stress release in knowing and accepting one's limitations. One of the serious problems in some congregations and with many good, sincere Christians is that they are spread so thin that they lose much of their effectiveness. Only a godlike person would think he knows how and is able to do everything there is to do.

(4) A person may discover that there is stress release in choosing not to accept any new responsibilities for a given period of time. Taking responsibility for oneself has a way of freeing

one and creating a relaxed and peaceful feeling at the same time. This suggestion is not to encourage Christians to be less active. Fewer assignments do not necessarily suggest that a person is not functioning in a more creative and productive manner than he did previously.

(5) An individual may find stress release in critically analyzing his current responsibilities in terms of the following:
   (a) How interesting they are to him intellectually, emotionally, and doctrinally.
   (b) How suited they are to him personally, vocationally, and spiritually.
   (c) Whether they meet his needs adequately and appropriately.

If a person selects responsibilities which **interest** him, which **suit** him best, and which **meet his needs** at **his desired level**, he will **feel less stress** and **tension**. Furthermore, he will be more productive, and perhaps he will not grow weary in doing good.

A Leader May Not Listen to Others Because He Is Afraid of Criticism

Solomon said, "Do not pay attention to every word people say, or you may hear your servant cursing you—for you know in your heart that many times you yourself have cursed others" (Ecclesiastes 7:21,22). A leader may be afraid he will hear others saying and doing the same things (at least in principle) that he says or does. He may not want to be dishonest with himself; therefore, he may be afraid to listen to others for fear he will hear himself in what they say.

There are at least four essential reasons (which are interrelated) why a leader may be afraid of criticism. One is he may feel **he is not an effective leader if people criticize him**. But Jesus said, "Woe to you when all men speak well of you, for that is how their fathers treated the false prophets" (Luke 6:26). This is not to suggest that a leader should seek to be controversial, but it is to say that he will be criticized. He may be criticized because group members do not understand what he is trying to do. Also, leading involves changing, which involves people's giving up that with which they have become comfortable and in which they feel secure. In changing, there is a certain amount of risk which can create anxiety, fear, frustration, and anger. To avoid facing and working through these feelings, a person may turn to criticizing his leaders. The degree and length of criticism depends on several things, such as the following:

(1) The degree and duration of criticism will be minimized if a leader does not become defensive and retaliate, but instead really listens to the criticisms with the intention of helping the individual who is doing the criticizing to come to a clearer understanding of himself as well as whatever he is criticizing.

(2) There is less criticism of a particular change if the people involved are accustomed to change.

(3) The more **personal** the change, the more intense the criticism, because the person's anxiety is greater due to his increased sense of personal threat.

(4) The clarity of the proposed change to the people, as far as who and what are involved and the benefits to be received, has profound influence on the extent and duration of the criticism.

(5) The depth of trust which a group of people have for a leader also significantly influences the amount of criticism given, as well as its duration.

(6) Whether the people had been prepared for the proposed change is another significant factor. Were their feelings and thoughts ever considered? Were they allowed to process their feelings and thus work through them?

(7) If an error in judgment, attitude, or action has been made, the extent to which a leader can freely and honestly confess his mistake responsibly will determine the extent of criticism.

The alert and mature leader knows that no one is exempt from misunderstanding and misrepresentation—especially leaders. It is clear to the maturing leader that some criticism is just and constructive. On the other hand, some is made unjustly, the motive being to hurt the leader himself and/or to destroy his influence. He is keenly conscious that some misrepresent him by not telling all of the truth, or by telling part of the truth mixed with falsehood. Also, a person may by voice, inflection, and emotion convey the wrong impression, but the basic result is the same.

In dealing with criticism and using it to one's advantage, a leader must wisely appraise any criticism before accepting or rejecting it. A maturing leader knows that it is possible for a person to learn valuable truths about himself from his detractors. It is a true adage that any leader should beware when people always seem to speak well of him. However, a maturing leader makes a fetish neither of conformity nor nonconformity, but guards his own integrity and freedom of judgment.

A second reason why a leader may be **afraid of criticism** is that he has certain vulnerabilities of which he does not want just anyone to know. But the nature of leadership is such that any leading or lack of it **exposes** a leader's vulnerabilities to others.

A third reason why a leader may be **afraid of criticism** is that he may think that **people should accept him and the judgments he makes without question**. A leader may even think that for one to question his leadership means that individual disrespects him as a person as well as a leader. This attitude is relatively common in certain areas, and is an outgrowth of culture without a Scriptural basis. A leader may have grown up with the idea that **children are to be seen and not heard**, and that to question an authority figure (parent, leader, God) is equal to disrespect and/or rebellion. But Christ certainly questioned his Father. For example, "My God, my God, why have you forsaken me?" (Matthew 27:46) Questions and criticisms in and of themselves are not sinful; they do not indicate disrespect for leaders or rebellion against them.

Nonverbal communication is the most accurate way of determining whether a particular question or a specific criticism indicates disrespect or rebellion. However, before accurate interpretation of a criticism or a question can be made, a leader must have accepted and worked through his own feelings regarding whether he should be criticized or questioned. After he has done this and can truly accept questions and criticisms, he must then notice and be able to interpret the nonverbal communication which accompanies the verbal communication. To illustrate: A leader must be able to hear and see (without being so threatened that he closes his ears and eyes) the disrespect or rebellion in the person's voice, face, gestures, posture, and speech rate.

One subtle point that is very important here is that anxiety and anger often look alike and sometimes sound alike. It is easy for a leader to have an incorrect assumption regarding anxiety or anger. Also, it may be difficult for a leader to be aware of a person's anger at times. Anger and anxiety are sometimes disguised through a **whining, self-pitying voice**, or in **overly pious words and mannerisms**. Sometimes a person sounds too pious to be real.

Criticisms or questions in and of themselves are not disrespectful of leaders, nor do they indicate that the group members are rebelling against the leaders. The most accurate way of determining whether a criticism or question is disrespectful or rebellious is for a leader to know his own thoughts regarding criticism of leaders. Understanding and properly interpreting nonverbal communication, though complex and difficult, is important. Hence, a leader should be very discerning in listening and very cautious when he interprets.

A fourth reason why a leader may be **afraid of criticism** is that a leader **can interpret a criticism as meaning the person doing the criticizing is angry at the leader**. Since a leader may not understand the nature of anger (its causes and appropriate, responsible expressions), he may become anxious, defensive, and closed. When he reaches this point, he may not really want to listen to the person who is criticizing him. Although a particular person may not be angry while criticizing, it is nevertheless true that some people do not criticize unless they are angry. Many people are overly afraid of anger and try to avoid dealing with it if at all possible.

A Leader May Not Listen Because He Has Closed His Eyes, Ears, and Heart, and Therefore Has Become Hard-Headed and Hard-Hearted

A leader may not listen to a group member or the group as a whole because he was **hurt** in the past and fears being hurt again, and/or he was not taught how to look, listen, and understand another. Therefore he has closed his eyes and ears, and does not understand with his heart. Thus he is not able to turn and be healed. Having become hard-headed and hard-hearted, he refuses to listen to suggestions or criticisms (see Ezekiel 2:2-8, 3:4-9; Jeremiah 5:21; Isaiah 6:9,10; Matthew 13:13-15).

A Leader May Not Listen Because He Does Not Know How to Listen

Listening is a skill and, therefore, must be learned. The age, number of children, education, and wealth of a leader do not guarantee that he knows how to listen to another person. In fact, these factors have nothing to do **per se** with how to listen or whether a leader does listen.

It is very important for a leader to learn (and this should be a continual process) how to listen, as well as what to listen for while working with people. Holy Scripture makes this clear. Jesus said, "Therefore consider carefully **how** you listen" (Luke 8:18). He also said, "Consider carefully **what** you hear" (Mark 4:24). He continued, "With the measure you use it will be measured to you—and even more. Whoever has will be given more; whoever does not have, even what he has will be taken from him" (Mark 4:24,25). Solomon said, "He who answers before listening—that is his folly and his shame" (Proverbs 18:13). He also stated, "A fool finds no pleasure in understanding but delights in airing his own opinions" (Proverbs 18:2). Jesus said:

> *Though seeing, they do not see; though hearing, they do not hear or understand. In them is fulfilled the prophecy of Isaiah: "You will be ever hearing but never understanding; you will be ever seeing but never perceiving. For this people's heart has become calloused; they hardly hear with their ears, and they have closed their eyes. Otherwise they might see with their eyes, hear with their ears, understand with their hearts and turn, and I would heal them" (Matthew 13:13-15; Isaiah 6:9,10).*

Jeremiah proclaimed, "Hear this, you foolish and senseless people, who have eyes but do not see, who have ears but do not hear" (Jeremiah 5:21). The Lord informed Ezekiel of the same basic problem when he said, "Son of man, you are living among a rebellious people. They have eyes to see but do not see and ears to hear but do not hear, for they are a rebellious people" (Ezekiel 12:2).

There can be no genuine listening until a leader can accept a person for what he is (not whether he has Christian morals, financial means, or a prominent position). One who truly listens neither condemns nor condones what a person does. An effective listener listens assiduously with open eyes and ears, not just to the words but primarily to the **feelings** of the person. His feelings are being communicated through his facial expression, gestures, posture, speech rate, breathing rate, and tone of voice. The motive of the effective leader is to help a group member gain true insight into himself, or to reach the point where he **understands with his heart so that he can turn and be healed**. Granted, this type of interpersonal relationship and intrapersonal insight is difficult to accomplish, but it is not insurmountable. Nevertheless, before this can be a reality, a leader must take the **art of listening** seriously, study it diligently and critically, and practice it sagaciously and patiently.

References

Bion, W. R., **Experience in Groups** (New York: Basic Books, 1959).

Campbell, A., **The Christian System** (Nashville: Gospel Advocate Company, 1956).

Gibbard, G. S., and Hartman, J. J., "A Note on Fantasy Themes in the Evolution of Group Culture;" in G. S. Gibbard, J. J. Hartman, and R. D. Mann (Eds.) **Analysis of Groups** (San Francisco: Jossey-Bass, 1974).

Jones, J. A., **Counseling Principles for Christian Leaders** (Abilene, Texas: Quality Publications, 1982).

Kaplan, S. R., and Roman, M., "Phases of Development in an Adult Therapy Group;" **International Journal of Group Psychotherapy**, 1963, **13**, 10-26.

Slater, P. E., **Microcosm: Structural, Psychological and Religious Evolution in Groups** (New York: John Wiley and Sons, Inc., 1966).

7 A Leader May Need To Be A God.

"God, I thank you that I am not like all other men ..."

(Luke 18:11)

Everyone Uses Some of the Following Tactics to Some Degree at One Time or Another

The defense tactics which shall be given will to some degree apply to all individuals (Salzman, 1980). They can be positive and constructive for a person. These tactics are not unhealthy in and of themselves. It is the **degree** to which they are **interwoven** and to which they **control** an individual's **thoughts** and **behaviors** which makes them unhealthy.

An **obsession** is a persistent and ritualized thought pattern. When a person is **obsessed**, he is preoccupied with thoughts in which he really is not interested, but which he finds impossible to get out of his mind. These strange thoughts may **compel** an individual to action which he does not enjoy, but nevertheless **feels forced to do**.

A **compulsion** is a consistent ritualized behavior pattern. One of the ways a Christian has of defending against certain thoughts and behaviors is to displace them with religious rituals and rules. A person may obsessively and compulsively think about and comply with religious rituals and rules as a way of protecting himself.

Some Things Which Influence a Person to Think He Is a God

An individual who needs to be a god began developing his defense tactics early in his life. Various traumatic experiences brought on by inconsistent, over-critical, ridiculing, rejecting, or even abandoning parents as well as other causes, such as various losses (friends, pets, important objects) or illness may have created anxiety and uncertainty. Siblings, peers, and heroes (like teachers and coaches) may have contributed to an individual's anxiety, uncertainty, and insecurity. Added to this may have been physical poverty, financial crises, and other uncontrollable painful circumstances in one's life as he developed. In addition, he may not have had parents and important others to create a safe environment in which to be vulnerable, share his pain, process it, and creatively learn from his experiences.

The person may have begun consciously or unconsciously inventing ways to avoid his pain and make himself completely safe and invincible to anxiety and uncertainty in his life. This being true, he became **obsessed** with thoughts which led to **compulsions** by which he could protect himself from being anxious, vulnerable, insecure, and uncertain. Therefore, he developed thought patterns and ritualistic behaviors which he thought would guarantee him the protection he needed.

Each one of the tactics he developed was **designed to keep him from being aware of his feelings** and therefore to enable him to avoid them. The leader who needs to be a god **does not experience his feelings**. This is not to say that he is not aware of having feelings at times. Emotions emerge to his awareness only under severe circumstances (such as a death of an important person); when they emerge, he does not experience them. He immediately begins to use tremendous amounts of mental and emotional energy to suppress them or move away from them. Two frequently-used ways of doing so are changing the subject being discussed and thinking of something else—sometimes with deep concentration. Having decided to block out his emotions because they were so painful, he never learned how to process them and thus experience the healthy effect which comes when feelings are worked through. He is obviously aware neither of his feelings nor the feelings of others. As he continues to block out painful feelings (such as anxiety, embarrassment, insecurity, and guilt), he cannot experience in a deep sense and for long periods of time his positive emotions.

Dedication Should Not Be Confused with Obsession

The obsessive-compulsive individual, through elaborate devices of avoiding commitments and decisions, has not learned the possibility of failure. He avoids being aware of his imperfection, fallibility, and humanness. The dedicated individual freely selects the idea or cause to which he commits his skills and interests. When one is obsessed, though, he is **imprisoned** and unable to choose freely.

A Leader Who Needs to Be a God Thinks He Is Omniscient

The leader who needs to be a god cannot acknowledge his very limited knowledge. Such an acknowledgment would put him in touch with his anxiety about not being knowledgeable in many areas. One should keep in mind that a person develops the omniscient tactic to protect himself from his feelings of anxiety and uncertainty. This type of individual concludes that if he only knew more and tried harder, he would one day know everything. Therefore, his obsession with knowledge stimulates more obsessional defenses.

The godlike leader's striving for omniscience causes him to overemphasize the rational element in himself. He often overestimates his intellectual capacity and its magical possibilities, and sometimes confuses thinking with achieving.

If one needs to be omniscient, he automatically sets himself up as a god and thus is not open for growth. Since he knows everything, who could teach him anything—except, perhaps, another person he views as being a god. He is the kind of person who likes to think that what is wrong with everybody else is that they are not listening to him.

A person may not be this open and frank, but his omniscience comes through in ways which are more subtle, some of which are as follows:

(1) Everyone must accept his view about everything, or they are wrong. While he may not see this, his behavior affirms this stance. He may change his opinion while he is developing his viewpoint, but once he sees his position as being fully developed, he will not change.

(2) He usually insists that everything from teaching to social activities be done **exactly** the way **it has always been done**.

(3) The level of teaching (even though the class members may have been in the church thirty years) emphasizes knowing dates, persons, and places, which is usually done through a simple drill, fill in the blanks, or true and false questions.

(4) He insists on a ritualized way of doing everything; for example, two songs, a prayer, another song and the sermon.

(5) The method of Bible study is a ritual which has to be repeated exactly the same way every time.

(6) Since he thinks he knows everything and everything is done in a ritualized pattern (and to be a member of that group one must conform to the rituals), there is no need to ask for suggestions from others because nothing is to be either learned or changed in that congregation. He may ask for suggestions but then quickly ignore them. If they are too **out of line,** he will rebuke or ridicule the person who made the suggestion. He may respond to the suggestion by an elaborate but very ritualized method of explaining that either it is wrong or it just would not work here anyway.

A Leader Who Needs to Be a God Thinks He Is Omnipotent

The leader who needs to be a god not only must know everything but must be all-powerful. Obviously, any leadership role is a powerful one. However, the godlike leader needs his power to control, dominate, and possess his subjects. Group members are not seen as individuals who need to be encouraged in growing so that they think and decide for themselves. They must remain **dependent** on the **wisdom of the leadership**.

There are a number of ways the godlike leader tries to maintain his omnipotence. Several methods of power control are as follows:

(1) The group members may hear frequent lessons and sermons designed to **frighten** them into **blind obedience**. Under such leadership, students are falsely taught that one should not doubt or question what is being taught. It is implied, if not explicitly stated, that questioning is equivalent to disrespect. Doubting is seen as a lack of faith and its acknowledgment as the destruction of one's faith. The leader who needs to be a god does not understand that questioning and doubting are healthy means of growing and strengthening one's trust and confidence. Such is healthy if the environment allows one to feel comfortable in raising his questions and sharing his doubts, and then to experience their being accepted and processed.

The godlike leader can be deceptive at this point because the impression can be given that here with this congregation is where one can come and reason. The seeker may soon find that only certain questions and doubts can be raised, and they must be raised in a certain manner and the ritualistic answers accepted.

If the seeker is persistent in wanting more, the leader may manifest his power through ignoring, ridiculing, and threatening him. Sometimes the power is exerted through the leader's equating his particular response as being God's response, and he may say, "God said it and that settles it." Fear is a powerful force which the godlike leader uses to maintain his power.

(2) Another method of power control which the godlike leader uses is that of ridicule. If a group member is not complying as the leader desires, the leader may simply ridicule or put down the group member in front of the group. This may be done in a very sarcastic manner. The leader who is skilled at this also effectively reinforces his verbal ridicule with nonverbal communication.

(3) A leader may exercise his control through rejecting a group member. This rejection may be verbal or nonverbal. Very often it is primarily nonverbal. The group member is ignored by the leader or other group members, is not invited to other group activities, and is not asked to teach or participate in public worship service. Of course, the group member may even be disfellowshipped publicly.

(4) Another way a godlike leader frequently exercises his power is through attempting to convince the group members that he is omniscient. This is usually done in a subtle manner each time the group is assembled.

The godlike leader produces a group of either passive, compliant, apathetic followers, or hostile and rebellious ones. Often the godlike leader will cause a church to split or disintegrate completely in attempting to maintain his control.

A Leader Who Needs to Be a God Is Certainly Grandiose

Grandiosity is the result of one who thinks he is omniscient and omnipotent. Paul said, "Do not think of yourself more highly than you ought" (Romans 12:3). The leader who needs to be a god never learned where to draw the line between having healthy self-esteem and being a god.

Having such grandiose ideas of himself, he cannot afford to be close to the group members and to model his humanness for them. Thus, he cannot really help the group members to grow individually and as a group. The extreme of his grandiosity is seen in that he may eventually become psychotic—out of touch with reality altogether.

A Leader Who Needs to Be a God Avoids Feelings

It should be understood that a person develops the tactics of omniscience, omnipotence, and grandiosity to avoid his anxiety, insecurity, and uncertainty. Thus, feelings (both painful and pleasant) are repressed, suppressed, denied, displaced, or projected onto others. (See chapter three, especially the section on **defense mechanisms**.)

The leader who needs to be a god cannot be truly effective in helping group members develop their whole persons because he does not accept and process his own emotions. Emotions are an innate part of a person, and one **cannot be fully a person** without accepting and experiencing them.

A group is made up of individuals, and being an individual is, in part, being emotional. Thus, as individuals, the group members will have feelings toward each other. Conflict is inherent within a person or a group. There cannot be personal or group conflict, though, without emotions being involved. The leader or the group members may not be aware of them, but feelings are inherent in personal or group conflict. Therefore, intrapersonal and interpersonal conflict cannot be resolved without feelings being accepted and processed. Furthermore, the group and its members are strengthened as feelings are accepted and processed.

A leader who needs to be a god denies and avoids his feelings, although he is actually caught between fear and rage. He is afraid of his anger. On the one hand, he is afraid of God and coming to grips with Him. On the other hand, he is angry with God. He may occasionally acknowledge his anxiety towards God, but seldom, if ever, will he acknowledge his anger for God. He may project his fear and rage onto others, and he often uses his religion to reinforce his obsessions. He becomes **obsessed** with a **works** and/or **doctrine** salvation (although he may deny it), which is void of genuine faith, hope, and love.

In addition, a leader who needs to be a god is limited in his ability to teach such dynamic concepts as trust, hope, love, and mercy. He may be able to give a clear etymological meaning of these words, but they have both an objective and an emotional dimension. These words are also developmental, and the power of them in a particular group member's life is developed not only as he understands the derived meaning of them, but also as he has experienced them in relationships. For example, Paul said, "I have been reminded of your sincere faith, which first lived in your grandmother Lois and in your mother Eunice, and I am persuaded, now lives in you also" (2 Timothy 1:5). As faith is developmental, so is hope, because the Hebrews writer said, "Now faith is being sure of what we hope for and certain of what we do not see" (Hebrews 11:1). Love likewise is developmental and has an emotional dimension. John said, "If anyone says, 'I love God,' yet hates his brother, he is a liar. For anyone who does not love his brother, whom he has seen, cannot love God, whom he has not seen" (1 John 4:20). As Paul defines love in 1 Corinthians 13:4-8, it is clear that there is an emotional dimension to each expression. Mercy carries with it the idea of being able to get inside of another so as to see, hear, and feel as that person does. So, obviously mercy has both a developmental aspect and an emotional dimension. Jesus said, "Blessed are the merciful, for they will be shown mercy" (Matthew 5:7; see also Jones, **Counseling Principles for Christian Leaders**, pp. 39-46).

It is clear that God wants the total person (Luke 10:25-28). As described in this passage, the total person is heart, soul, strength, and mind. Thus, if the total person is to be developed, one's emotions must be accepted and processed. A leader who needs to be a god, though, is limiting his own growth as well as that of the group members. While he may grow some intellectually, he definitely is not going to grow emotionally because he denies and avoids his feelings.

A Leader Who Needs to Be a God Is Stubborn

A godlike leader views himself as reasonable. If he is a Christian, he may take great pride in quoting such passages as "Come now, let us reason together" (Isaiah 1:18). He likes to talk about being set for the defense of the gospel (Philippians 1:16). In reality, he may have learned some **pat answers** for why he believes and acts the way he does. The reasons he does give are very simplistic and rigid. His overly simplistic world view fits in with his need to be omniscient and omnipotent. If one thinks he knows everything and has all power, he, of necessity, has to develop a simplistic philosophy. Since he thinks everything is black or white and very simple, he applies his narrow and rigid view to all of life.

The godlike leader's stubbornness is seen when he is challenged to consider new ideas or different questions. Most of his reasons for doing things are unconscious. The anxiety raised by different concepts flushes out his stubbornness, which he developed as a defense tactic to avoid his anxiety. He manifests that, after all, he is not a very reasonable person.

A stubborn leader is usually an impulsive leader. He **reacts** instead of **acts**. Most of his decisions are made on **impulse** or by **default** instead of by **reason**. Contrary to what the godlike leader thinks, he is much more irrational than rational.

Stubbornness suggests that one has not thought out and come to his own valid conclusions. It suggests that one should not expect to be accountable for his decisions and, therefore, should not be questioned regarding them. He expects the group members to follow his dictates blindly. He may call his dictates suggestions, but if a group member persists in challenging him, it will soon be discovered that his suggestions are really orders.

A Leader Who Needs to Be a God Operates More by Fear than by Faith

A godlike leader thinks he walks by faith (2 Corinthians 5:7), but in reality, he is controlled far more by fear than by genuinely trusting himself, others, and God. He does not talk about his fear; it gets expressed in subtle but powerful ways. Instead of saying he is afraid, analyzing his fear, and giving reasons for being frightened, he is more likely to say something like the following: "We cannot do that here," "That costs too much," "The interest rate is going up," "Somebody may get the wrong impression," "Why can't we accept things like they've always been?" "Why do we have to have something new going on all the time?" "I am not for anything which might be a stumbling block in someone else's way," "We just need more sound preaching," or "My kids were never played with and taken on retreats." The list goes on, but, most often, feelings which underlie these expressions are never accepted and processed.

A godlike leader, instead of walking by faith, fears change of any kind. He is afraid of personal, marital, and congregational growth. He is afraid of new ideas. He is afraid of going to hell and of his own feelings. He is afraid to be angry or to be compassionate. He is afraid to be tender and fearful of being tough. He is afraid to be kind, and he is fearful of warmth. He is afraid to live and afraid to die.

Controlled by his fear, which he does not acknowledge, accept, and process, a godlike leader does not deeply trust; therefore, he does not learn how to love. Paul accurately describes him when he says:

> *If I speak in the tongues of men and of angels, but have not love, I am only a resounding gong or a clanging cymbal. If I have the gift of prophecy, and can fathom all mysteries and all knowledge, and if I have a faith that can move mountains, but have not love, I am nothing. If I give all I possess to the poor and surrender my body to the flames, but have not love, I gain nothing (1 Corinthians 13:1-3).*

A Leader Who Needs to Be a God Thinks He Is Perfect

One of the tactics a godlike leader develops is that of perfection. He develops this illusion to avoid his sins, real or imaginary. He may become so obsessed with carrying out rituals to avoid feeling sinful (dirty) that he actually becomes dirty. His religion may become very one-sided—obsessed with the evils of sin. His lectures and sermons may be a constant diet of dirt, the motives of which is to create fear, shame, and guilt in the members. He may try to avoid his dirt through focusing on the sins of others (Matthew 7:1-5). He can spend long periods of time compulsively giving reasons as to why others should not dirty themselves, while consciously or unconsciously feeling dirty himself. A leader who needs to be a god may become such an extremist that there is no joy, happiness, peace, fulfillment, and real meaning in his life. Solomon said:

> *In this meaningless life of mine I have seen both of these: a righteous man perishing in his righteousness, and a wicked man living long in his wickedness. Do not be overrighteous, neither be overwise—why destroy yourself? Do not be overwicked, and do not be a fool—why die before your time? It is good to grasp the one and not let go of the other. The man who fears God will avoid all extremes (Ecclesiastes 7:15-18).*

A Leader Who Needs to Be a God Cannot Experience Complete Forgiveness

Much emphasis in Bible classes and sermons is placed on God's forgiving a person. I think the greatest problem regarding forgiveness lies not with God, but with the individual himself. Whether or not a person was reared by forgiving parents has a profound influence on one's ability to forgive himself. Another important factor is whether a person grew up in forgiving groups (such as a church). There are a number of other related factors regarding whether one can truly forgive himself. Two significant ones are as follows:

(1) Was the child taught truth correctly and understandably on his developmental level?

(2) When he made a mistake, were these the results:
  - (a) Was he aided by his parents, teachers, and group members to see and accept his mistake?
  - (b) Was he forgiven by them, and did he experience their forgiveness?

To the degree that one can answer the above questions affirmatively, and to the degree that he has a precisely defined, adequate, and realistic value system, he can forgive himself as often as is necessary. He also will have no serious problem with accepting the fact that God can forgive him of any sin if he will repent of it and confess it.

A leader needs to understand that forgiveness is only genuinely learned in the experience of ongoing relationships. A group member who grew up in relationships where he never experienced forgiveness, or where forgiveness was partial, haphazard, and inconsistent, will have difficulty forgiving himself. In fact, he very likely will not forgive himself and others nor be able to accept God's forgiveness without some professional psychotherapy assistance. To tell a group member who has been so deprived that he must forgive is wasting words, and this type of response will most likely increase his problem. A group member, if significantly helped, must be aided by other group members and the leader, usually over a long period of time, before he really can learn forgiveness. Depending upon one's age and deprivation, it most likely will take a therapy-type relationship for a group member to learn this. What initially could have been a natural and relatively easy process will now be quite frightening, very painful, and time-consuming for him.

There are at least three reasons why a leader who needs to be a god cannot experience complete forgiveness, and they are as follows:

(1) He thinks he is perfect; therefore, he does not sin. If he does not sin, how could he experience forgiveness?

(2) Forgiveness is much more than an apology; therefore, for one to simply say "I am sorry" does not necessarily mean he has been forgiven or feels he is forgiven. An apology may not be an apology. A leader who needs to be a god, if pressed, may say something like "If I have sinned" or "I may have sinned"; such is not an apology. An intellectual or academic response is not an apology. A true apology comes from insight into and acceptance of the fact that one has sinned. A genuine apology is also a confession of the feelings of guilt and regret.

(3) Guilt is a state or condition which has an emotional component. One can be guilty, but not necessarily feel guilty. One cannot feel (experience) forgiveness, though, by only responding cognitively or by just changing the mind and

behavior. A person can change his state or condition, but guilt is not fully removed until an individual has processed his feelings. Since a leader who needs to be a god **denies his feelings**, he cannot experience complete forgiveness.

A leader who needs to be a god creates problems for himself as well as the group members. This is true because he attempts to defy reality—the reality that there is only one true God.

References

Salzman, L., **Treatment of the Obsessive Personality** (New York: Jason Aronson, 1980).

Jones, J. A., **Counseling Principles for Christian Leaders** (Abilene, Texas: Quality Publications, 1982).

8

Reasons Why Members Need Their Leaders To Be Gods.

"Come, make us gods who will go before us."

(Exodus 32:1)

The God Symbol

In this book, I frequently use the words **god** or **godlike**. Therefore, I think it is important to explain what I mean by this symbol. An individual is attributing to a leader godlike qualities when he believes that the leader possesses the following characteristics:

(1) **Magical powers inherent in his person**. Often ministers, elders, and others are thought to have this characteristic. There have been many individuals through my thirty years of ministry who have shared with me that they thought the minister or elder was **superhuman**. Sometimes ministers and elders communicate these thoughts to their followers, either intentionally or not, by the terminology they use in referring to themselves. I have heard many times through the years that members felt their minister or elders were so spiritual that they were not really human. In the eyes of some, just being a Christian college president or the head of a Bible department in a Christian college means that a person has some kind of super power. It should be understood that it is natural, and therefore very easy, for an individual to project onto another those qualities or traits (powers) he does not have but wants or needs, and imagines that the other does have because of his education and position.

(2) **Omniscience or omnipotence as a result of being a scholar or an expert**. I have never heard anyone say that another minister or expert was a god, but I have heard many times through the years such statements as "What else could be said; he said it all" or "You mean you would disagree with...? He has been a preacher or teacher for 'x' number of years." If a person has written a book (it does not really matter what type—a commentary, a collection of sermon outlines, etc.), in the eyes of some, he has become omniscient. The individual who has a doctorate degree (especially an earned one) is often seen as being omniscient, regardless of whether or not he is speaking in his specific area.

(3) **The ability to perform tricks, magic, or even miracles because of his expertise**. How many times have elders

thought that the answer to a particular problem was having an expert come in and give a few lectures or sermons and the problem would be solved. There are leaders in the church who are constantly looking for easy, painless, and effortless solutions to their problems. In other words, if an **expert** is called in, he can, through **trickery** and **magic**, **make things all right**. Elders do not say this, but their actions and the way they talk about such things clearly indicate that they think an expert can defy hard core reality. This is one reason why elders, ministers, and congregations are so receptive to fads and gimmicks.

Infantile Members Need to See Their Leaders as Gods

Just as parents were initially seen as gods, so are leaders in the beginning stage of the group. The new convert sees the one who taught him the truth as a god. When a congregation first hires a minister, it sees him as a god. When a congregation selects elders, it initially sees them as gods. When a person changes congregations, he sees his new leaders as gods. In the beginning stage of any group, the members attribute to their leaders **godlike qualities**—they tend to see them as **omniscient and omnipotent**. This happens regardless of whether the leaders are aware that the members have such fantasies of them, or whether they reject these projections or foster them verbally or nonverbally. Being "babes in Christ" (1 Peter 2:2) and **emotionally regressive** (Scheidlinger, 1968), it is only natural for the group members to project onto their leaders the qualities they desire them to have.

This phenomenon is not unique to the twentieth century. Cornelius fell before Peter as a representative of God (Acts 10:22-26). John fell before the feet of the angel (messenger) to worship him (Revelation 22:8,9). Simon the Sorcerer convinced the people of Samaria ("high and low") that he was the divine power (Acts 8:9-25). The people of Lystra identified Paul and Barnabas with Zeus (the god of the sky) and Hermes (the spokesman of the gods) (Acts 14:8-18). Peter, John,

Paul, and Barnabas discouraged being deified, while Simon the Sorcerer deeply desired and encouraged deification.

Insecurity, Anxiety, and Confusion Cause Members to See Their Leaders as Gods

It is comforting to be identified with someone whom one thinks can provide all his needs in a safe and nonthreatening environment. Thus, it becomes very easy for the new member or the immature individual to project omniscience and omnipotence onto his leaders. It is not difficult for a new convert to regress emotionally to a preschool level and thus attribute to his leaders those qualities commensurate with this developmental level. This should not be considered strange, because Paul saw the Corinthians as infants, not adults (1 Corinthians 3:1,2). Paul also stated, "When I was a child, I talked like a child, I thought like a child, I reasoned like a child. When I became a man, I put childish ways behind me" (1 Corinthians 13:11). But how many times when under pressure has the leader said to another, "Quit acting like a child!" The point is, all individuals emotionally regress at different times in their lives. When they regress, they act and talk in a manner commensurate with the developmental age to which they have regressed.

A Person Behaves Differently in a Group

I often hear someone say, "He acts differently in a group than he does when I am with him alone." It is true that a person thinks, feels, and acts differently in a group than he does in one-to-one relationships. An individual also thinks, feels, and acts differently when alone than when he is in relationship to one other person. The difference may be very minor, or he may not be aware of it, but nevertheless it exists. It is more difficult for a person to **be himself** at the beginning of a group than in its later development. This is **not** true if the **group's** and the leader's norm is for a person to **lose his individuality within the group**; that is, to lose one's ability to think and act for oneself, especially when such thoughts and actions are in conflict with those of other members. Peer pressure can be tremendous. Sometimes the pressure can exist more in the individual's own mind than in reality. In other words, a member may think the group would apply pressure to him if he voiced an objection or a difference. The group norm mentioned above can be operating, though, with or without the leader's or group's being aware of it.

The more **confused or lost** a person is, the more he may need to see his leaders as being gods. Being lost suggests that one is unaware of who he is, where he fits, and where he is going; thus, his anxiety is raised. If a person was overprotected while growing up, or if he experienced extreme anxiety when he was lost, he may tend to deny being lost earnestly as an adult to avoid his anxiety. Being lost, though, automatically stirs up earlier feelings which may be outside one's awareness; the less aware one is, the more rigid are his defenses and the more persistent is his denial.

The level of anxiety which one feels in his confusion is proportional to such factors as the following:

(1) The level his anxiety reached in similar situations when he was growing up.

(2) How emotionally and intellectually accepting of his being lost his parents were.

(3) How effectively they taught him to **find himself** as well as **his way** at the times when he was lost while growing up.

(4) How open he was to his experiences of being lost and to what he learned from those experiences. Solomon said, "I applied my heart to what I observed and learned a lesson from what I saw" (Proverbs 24:32).

One of the benefits which comes from being lost is the discovery of finding self and others, and learning that one's environment is not as threatening as he had thought. After all, one who can accept being lost and can find himself and his way discovers new and richer dimensions in himself and his relationships. This cumulative experience is a source of encouragement for one to be open to being lost at times.

One of the basic purposes of Christianity is for a person to find himself. The lost son could not deal with himself in reality until he "came to his senses" (Luke 15:17). Coming to one's senses may be difficult and time-consuming because of the depth of one's confusion or state of being lost. Isaiah stated that a person could be so lost or confused that he could call evil good or good evil, put darkness for light and light for darkness, put bitter for sweet and sweet for bitter (Isaiah 5:20). Solomon said, "There is a way that seems right to a man, but in the end it leads to death" (Proverbs 14:12; 16:25). Jeremiah said, "I know, O Lord, that a man's life is not his own; it is not for man to direct his steps" (Jeremiah 10:23). Jesus said, "Whoever finds his life will lose it, and whoever loses his life for my sake will find it" (Matthew 10:39; see Matthew 16:25, Mark 8:35, and Luke 9:24). It seems obvious that one of the easiest things a person can do is to become lost from himself, others, and God. Life and self are inseparable—to find one is to find the other.

It is a fact that a person will do things in a group that he will not do with one other individual or alone. Of course, the reverse is true. An individual often loses his individuality in a group, even though he may struggle to be himself. His struggle may be felt more internally than verbalized to the group. He may lack insight into the nature of his conflict, as well as how to articulate it to the group. He may be just too afraid or embarrassed to risk sharing it.

It is no accident that a person thinks, feels, and acts differently in a group than in a one-to-one relationship or even when by himself. This happens because of complex powerful forces acting within the individual and the group. Furthermore, this is characteristic of a person from early childhood throughout one's life. Some reasons for this are as follows:

(1) It is difficult to be oneself and be related to another at the same time. As the number of persons in the group increases, so does the complexity of the group dynamics and the difficulty of relating to others as well as oneself.

(2) One's degree of self-awareness, self-acceptance, self-control, self-confidence, and self-expression (verbal and nonverbal) are influential factors as to what a person will be like in the group, as well as what he feels about himself.

(3) The group norm certainly influences what an individual will or will not say in a group, as well as when and how he will say it.

Who Has the Power in This Group?

In the beginning stages of any group, the members will see their leaders as gods, whether the leaders wish for them to or not. However, group pathology begins to develop when leaders need (consciously or unconsciously) the group members to remain infants. Leaders have ways of communicating these desires through such statements as the following:

(1) "He said it all." (Wisdom is inherent in the leader; therefore, no group member could contribute anything of significance.)

(2) "The leaders have decided" (without the members being involved in the decision-making process or knowing the process through which the leaders arrived at their decision).

The illusion that the leaders are gods is maintained through studying the subject with the same material in the same way for years on end. It is regrettable that in many adult classes, they have never gotten beyond true-and-false and fill-in questions after years of study. Leaders who operate on this educational level do not understand their students' need to grow, and that growth comes through questioning and discovering that their leaders, like their parents, are not gods.

Leaders who are close-minded, rigid, and authoritarian do not want the group members to question or disagree with them. This is a way they keep the group members infants; both they and their followers can further the illusion that the leaders are gods. This over-dependent relationship leads to hostility and fights. The fighting may move frequently and abruptly from in-group fighting to attacking what is often perceived as the outside enemy. Usually the enemy is a **straw person** created in the imagination of the group (especially its leaders) and easily devoured. This fight-flight pattern is a way of avoiding the intrapersonal and interpersonal issues within the group.

The group naturally deals with exclusion-inclusion issues (who is saved and who is lost, who is a member of the church and who is not). Every group has membership requirements, but doggedly and continually talking about these requirements can foster the godlike illusion and further breed hostile dependency. The group must do more than emphasize its membership requirements and its exclusive relationship if it is to grow. The Hebrews writer and Peter emphasized the importance of growth (Hebrews 5:12-14; 6:1,2; 1 Corinthians 3:1-9; 1 Peter 2:2; 2 Peter 3:18).

As a result of growth and discovering that a leader is not omniscient and omnipotent but, in fact, is at times weak, inconsistent, and contradictory, members seek to overthrow their leader or become very critical of him. Being disappointed and disillusioned in their leaders, they may respond in the following ways:

(1) They may internalize their anger. The internalizing of their anger may be seen in sulking, apathy, and depression.

(2) They may express their anger passively by being late for services and/or reducing their contribution.

(3) They may allow leaders to plan programs for them and then sabotage the programs. This is one reason why so many programs fail or have minimum effectiveness. The sabotaging of programs can be done through a variety of means, two of which are as follows:
   (a) By not responding when a leader asks them to respond.
   (b) By accepting responsibility and not following through.

(4) They may quietly leave the group (the church).

(5) They may attack their leaders openly, becoming very critical and defiant of them and their leadership.

(6) They may become spiritually promiscuous and then be indifferent to their leaders' rebukes. Thus, there may be an ongoing fight with the leaders for years.

The reasons why members need gods are initially healthy. They become unhealthy when their leaders, needing to be gods, do not provide adequate nutrition and proper exercise to enable the members to grow into adulthood.

References

Scheidlinger, S., "The Concept of Regression in Group Psychotherapy," **International Journal of Group Psychotherapy**, 1968, 18, 3-20.

9 Qualities Of An Effective Leader

"There is a time for everything, and a season for every activity under heaven ... a time to weep and a time to laugh ... a time to embrace and a time to refrain ... a time to be silent and a time to speak, a time to love and a time to hate ..."

(Ecclesiastes 3:1,4,5,7,8)

Traits Are Interrelated

The qualities discussed in this chapter are interrelated. I see them as basic essentials, although no single leader possesses them fully. Therefore, he would need to grow in them continually. In addition, there are other qualities he should possess and in which he should grow. For example, he should **model** openness, warmth, honesty, respect, concern, acceptance, responsibility, and perseverance as he facilitates, nurtures, stimulates, manages, and structures the group.

An Effective Group Leader Is Not Controlled by His Past

A leader who has accepted and processed his past neither feels guilty nor blames himself, his parents, nor others for the mistakes he has made. Furthermore, he has taken responsible action for the mistakes he made, processed his feelings, and forgiven himself. Therefore, he does not feel embarrassed or guilty about what happened in the past. This does not mean he approves of his past attitude or behavior. The degree to which he has worked through his past determines what he is able to share comfortably and without embarrassment from his own past and present if it is appropriate to do so. He has worked through his feelings to the point that, though how he was formed or deformed still influences him, he is not controlled or absolutely determined by his past, but is freed up to make clearer choices in the present.

A leader's residual problems can cause more difficulties in a group situation than in a one-to-one situation because they are so quickly and sharply brought out by the group impact. A leader may say quite upsetting things without being aware of doing so because of his own blind spots, and because a good follow-up on the effects of his remarks may not be possible. It is an established fact that what one may say to one person in a particular situation might prove helpful, but the same response might prove to be very upsetting for another person.

A leader may steer clear of certain problems of the group members because of his own blind spots. Even if the group members should recognize certain problems within themselves and want to work on them, a leader might frustrate this by avoidance or defensive hostility. A leader who cannot be wholeheartedly frank because of his own difficulties with the situation will not likely ask such frankness from the members. He may not require the members to be candid because he would feel that he was being put in an indefensible and contradictory position. If a leader knows about his problems, the group situation could be constructively helpful to him. If he does not, especially if these problems are obvious to some of the group members, some rather unpleasant situations may arise. He might get the full impact of the group's exposure and criticism. Thus, he might become inhibited, frustrated, or irritated to the detriment of all concerned. Also, the group requires greater ability of a leader than does a one-to-one relationship. This is because of the wide, intense, and sudden shifts in mood toward the leader which are more likely to occur.

A leader may become attracted to groups to fulfill certain needs of which he is not aware. He may become involved with groups to cover up a feeling of incompetence with individuals. A group situation, rather than exposing, might entrench him in his own irrational drives because of the false pride he gets from it. In addition, to cover up his feelings of incompetence, he might inflate the results he obtains. Of course, this can also be done in regard to one-to-one situations. Therefore, a leader needs prior training and supervision before undertaking group work, as well as occasional training and quality supervision during the process of group work.

Obviously, the **group members and the leader bring their past with them**. It is largely the leader, though, who facilitates what will happen, especially in the earlier sessions. Much of what does or does not go on in the earlier sessions depends upon such factors as follow:

(1) The leader's training.

(2) His inner conflicts, or lack of them.

(3) His needs and interests.

(4) His ability to set structure.

(5) His contract with the group.

A leader who has not processed his inner conflicts and who does not understand group dynamics may not be able to receive the deification which the group bestows upon him. Furthermore, he may not use his power for effective edification and healing purposes.

A leader may aid the group in its development through his analogue reasoning and cryptic remarks. He also facilitates, nurtures, stimulates, manages, and structures the group. He is most effective if he maintains a balance in his tasks.

An Effective Leader Understands Group Dynamics

In any group, there are numerous forces taking place. Of course, the larger the group, the greater increase there is in the dynamics within the group. A skilled group leader is **alert** to these various forces. He seeks to **understand** and respond to them **appropriately** and **responsibly**. A skilled leader is aware that individual as well as group dynamics are constantly moving and are not static and stationary.

A leader should distinguish between his feelings and the group members' feelings. In fact, a danger for a leader can be ignorance of his own internal dynamics. It should be understood that a group member views the leader from the member's past experiences, as well as his present needs. A group member's feelings about the leader may reactivate old feelings toward other authority figures (such as parents or teachers). When these feelings are transferred to the leader, they may reactivate old feelings in the leader which he may countertransfer to the group member. He may be unaware of his countertransference and respond inappropriately.

A group member may be indifferent, unresponsive, and detached. These feelings are rooted in his character structure which has evolved from his past experiences. These feelings also reflect the influences of significant people in his life. The group member's character structure has a present dynamic of its own which is based on his inner conflicts as well as defensive solutions to conflicts. All these factors come into play in understanding a particular group member's complex reactions to the group leader. A group member's habitual reactions to people, which are based on his personal needs and conflicts, will be applied to feelings about the leader. A leader **facilitates, nurtures, stimulates,**

manages, and **structures** the group; these special roles stir feelings toward him in members of the group.

Group members symbolically find their father, mother, siblings, and important others in the group experience. If the group is structured properly, they have the opportunity to work through these relationship problems which tie the past with the present. The interpersonal contacts and transactions in the group can be helpful in improving the socialization of the members. They can learn what their effects on other people are and how they are affected by others. The various facets of people's relationship problems become evident in the group. Peak experiences in the group are moments of intense emotional expressions and interactions which reflect deep positive intrapsychic and interpersonal communication. When they occur, the group members and the leader may feel they have undergone a strong liberating experience.

Most people who have been affected by the competitive struggle in their world are conditioned to feel distrustful and guarded in their relationships with other people. In the group process, there is conflict between these old attitudes and the movement toward mutually constructive helpfulness, toward togetherness and closeness. A leader should recognize that changing is not easy, for it requires the reversal of many strongly-held patterns. Members even may be unaware of many of these patterns.

A leader should also be aware that the formation of alliances or subgroups is a phenomenon usually seen in the group process. Some members are relatively steady, while others shift constantly. Some individuals are drawn to each other on the basis of leadership qualities or dependency needs. Other alliances are based on mutual resistances and destructive patterns. These members are victims of hopelessness and cynicism. The alliance may be used as a method of taking power over the rest of the group. Some group members simply may share feelings of closeness and mutual warmth.

The character traits of the group members are revealed in their relations toward each other during the group process. A **dependent** individual will try to please and appease the others. The constant drive to dominate and control is the mark of the **aggressive** member. The group member who seems to be indifferent to and withdrawn from the others is suffering from **detachment**. The **narcissist** tries to charm, but cannot be relied upon for any reciprocal relationships. A **vindictive** person throws pointed verbal barbs and hostile criticism whenever he has the opportunity. A **resigned** member may sit silently, sometimes with his eyes closed, not participating in the group discussion, or he may act out rebelliously by being late or absent.

Naturally, any of these traits provoke reactions in the other people. The group members each respond in their own particular ways, depending upon their own character structure and needs. Constant reality testing occurs during the group process. A group leader should encourage both an active interactional process and an increasing measure of trust in the integrity of the group. As people grow during the process, they feel more secure and can, therefore, let their guard down and talk more freely. In fact, they may reach the point where they can have frank verbal exchanges with others without being vulnerable and easily hurt. They also learn that, even if they feel hurt occasionally, they will heal; there will be another time, and relationships are constantly in an evolutionary process.

A group leader should be aware that people frequently prefer to talk about their own personal problems, usually current but sometimes tied in with the past. They hope to find answers and obtain some relief. Such people require encouragement to interact with other group members, and the group leader should be alert to opportunities to promote such interaction. On the other hand, there are people who react almost immediately to one or several other group members.

An Effective Leader Understands Transference and Countertransference

Transference is the phenomenon of projecting one's thoughts, feelings, and wishes from one's past onto the group leader and other group members (Durkin, 1964; Slavson, 1950). The group leader and other group members have come to **represent a person** (a parent, sibling, or other important individual) from a particular group member's past. The group leader and other group members are **reacted to as though they were people from the specific group member's past**. The feelings which are reactivated are usually sexual feelings, fear, embarrassment, anger, guilt, and affection. These reactions may be appropriate in childhood and in various stages of the group (see chapter 1), but they are inappropriate when acted out or not processed.

In a broad sense, transference also includes thoughts, feelings, and wishes which a group member had towards **places** and **situations** of the past. Current places and situations may be **similar** to past ones and may reactivate old thoughts, feelings, and wishes. Since people, places, and situations are interrelated in one's experiences, an individual may project his thoughts, feelings, and wishes from the past into the present.

Transference can happen immediately and in all types of relationships. It is not uncommon for someone to encounter a person who reminds him of an individual from his past. Upon remembering the person, place, and situation of the past, he may project revived thoughts, feelings, and wishes onto the stranger. Just seeing a new person or place may reactivate such feelings as eroticism, fear, embarrassment, anger, or affection toward a person or place in one's past. However, **the person** who is experiencing such feelings **may not be aware** that he is transferring thoughts, feelings, and wishes from the past into the present.

It should be understood that the term "transference" **does not** refer to reactions which are based on **reality factors** in the relationship between a group member and the leader or other members. For example, if a leader misses an appointment, group members would ordinarily be angry. This is not transference. The leader actually missed the meeting, and the group members are angry because of that fact. However, a reality experience can activate old thoughts, feelings, and wishes. For example, a leader's missing an appointment is a reality experience. A particular group member may (in addition to his current thoughts, feelings, and wishes toward the leader) transfer unresolved feelings toward other authority figures for having done similar things. Therefore, transference can be interrelated with reality factors.

When individuals become emotionally involved with each other, repressed unconscious material is revived. Since these thoughts, feelings, and wishes were not satisfactorily met in the past and are reactivated, one may seek gratification of them in the group. It should be understood that **talking out** (processing) feelings is necessary for individual and group growth, while **acting out** feelings can be destructive. Therefore, one group rule should be that members cannot **act out** their transferences (see p. 28).

Countertransference is the phenomenon of a leader projecting his thoughts, feelings, and wishes from his past onto a particular group member. The group member's personality, what he is sharing, or the situation, may represent people, places, and experiences in the leader's past. A group member may serve some need of the leader, such as alleviation of anxiety or mastery of guilt feelings. Passive masochistic wishes in the leader may cause him to accept a group member's accusation or mistreatment of him instead of causing him to confront and analyze this behavior. Unconscious aggression in the leader may lead him to boredom or overeagerness. A leader may, because of his suspicious attitude, get the group member to disclose what the leader does not want to see in himself. A leader who has a need mainly for narcissistic (selfish) gratification will see himself as a **magic healer**. This perception may lead him to be overly ambitious, and he may become hostile toward group members who do not **improve** as he wishes.

The degree to which a leader has processed his thoughts, feelings, and wishes of the past largely determines to what degree he can choose how to respond to the group member. Otherwise, he responds to the group member as he would have responded to someone in his past. For example, if a group member is angry at the leader because of what he represents from the member's past, the group leader who has not processed his feelings about being the object of someone's anger may respond either by becoming hostile and defensive, or by withdrawing or placating the group member.

It should be understood that transference and countertransference have to do with people, places, and events of the past. The feelings are projected into the present because the present is stirring up the past, of which both members and the leader may be unaware. One of the values of a leader's processing his past is that he can be more aware of the transference and countertransference which take place in a group almost constantly. When a leader is aware of the transference-countertransference phenomenon taking place, he is able to make some choices about how he will use his countertransference in the group. To illustrate, a group member may have become angry toward him and is expecting ridicule. If the leader chooses instead to respond in a warm, accepting manner, this can be therapeutic for the group member. On the other hand, if a leader is controlled by his past, he may simply react as the group member's father would have reacted. Thus, from that transaction, no emotional nor mental progress would be made.

My experience has taught me something of the significance of transference and countertransference. Therefore, I have serious questions about certain types of groups and group leaders because of the complexity of transference and countertransference. Some short-term **cure-all** groups may meet long enough to produce a transference in a group member, but then not be there to help him work through it effectively. Unless there is some type of transference and the opportunity to work through it, a group member is not likely to be helped much. In addition, a group leader may not be skilled enough to understand the nature of transference; as a result, through countertransference, he may confuse or hurt a group member even more. Nevertheless, there can be constructive uses of transference.

A religious leader who understands and is professionally involved in transference relationships within his congregation has a clearer understanding of the precise struggles in which his people are involved. He also is in a position to speak to these needs in sermons and Bible lessons, as well as to plan different types of small groups and other educational activities which can enable his people to mature.

The aim of the Law, as well as of Christ, was for a person to reach the point where he could love God with all his heart, soul, strength, and mind, and his neighbor as himself (Luke 10:25-27; 1 Timothy 1:5). Helping a person to reach maturity or wholeness is complicated, and requires considerable time and painstaking effort. This is especially true of an adolescent because he is in an identity search; until he finds himself and his purpose in life, he usually shifts back and forth between the following emphases:

(1) Loving God with his heart (feelings).

(2) Loving God with his soul (life—like Peter, at certain moments he feels he would give his life for Christ).

(3) Loving God with his strength (at times working very hard and enthusiastically).

(4) Loving God with his mind (intellect—at times he really gets involved in reading and studying).

So often these one-sided emphases are spasmodic and haphazard. Also, it is possible for one or more of these areas (heart, soul, strength, mind) to be neglected for long periods of time, and even ignored completely. A person is usually in his middle or late twenties or early thirties before he can believe what is true, wholeheartedly, in a really deep sense (Allport, 1950). Since this is the case, each congregation's teachers and curriculum frequently should receive a serious objective and exhaustive study to determine what corrections and improvements are to be made in the educational process. When the whole person (heart, life, strength, mind) is spasmodically and haphazardly dealt with in religious education, or parts of him (such as his heart) are minimized or ignored in Bible study, sermons, and religious activities, he is not likely to become whole or mature.

Developing one's mind and heart includes studying and understanding the mind and the emotions, as well as intellectual concepts and facts. Cultivating one's heart and mind also involves learning to express one's ideas and feelings clearly, tersely, and responsibly. In addition, the adolescent needs to distinguish clearly his various feelings and cultivate them in conjunction with his mind.

One of the basic needs of man is to be related in a loving, meaningful, purposeful, and responsible manner to others. Paul said, "For none of us lives to himself alone and none of us dies to himself alone" (Romans 14:7). After God had created man, he said, "It is not good for the man to be alone. I will make a helper suitable for him...for this reason a man will leave his father and mother and will be united to his wife, and they will become one flesh" (Genesis 2:18,24).

The physical attraction which adolescents experience are normal, good, and clean because this is the way God made human beings. However, it is imperative for teenagers to understand their dual nature—physical and spiritual. The biological or sexual drive will develop naturally , but the main point of concern for the adolescent should be to understand it, accept it, and responsibly use it in conjunction with his emotional, spiritual, or physical side.

Man is so made that if he does not develop his mind and heart properly and learn how to express both appropriately and adequately, he becomes perverted (broken, split, twisted). The degree of perversion is predicated upon the length of time, type of relationships, and a number of other casual factors. Being ignorant of one's feelings and how to express them appropriately, denying them, or feeling ashamed, guilty, and afraid of them and their legitimate expression only assures their being expressed in perverted ways.

A person's emotions need proper expression, but, if denied appropriate expression, they will eventually come out in disguised and perverted ways. This is why it is so important for parents and teachers to teach their children or students how to express themselves intellectually, emotionally, and religiously in a proper and responsible manner. In other words, intrapersonal and interpersonal communication on a deep level is a basic component of Christianity, and helps in a genuine and meaningful way to prevent the Christian from going to extremes intellectually, emotionally, socially, and sexually. Deep personal and interpersonal communication forces the group member and the leader to look at themselves honestly, to listen to themselves critically, and to understand themselves realistically. It forces them to struggle with expressing their true feelings and thoughts together in an open, honest, acceptable, and responsible manner.

Obviously, transference is involved in relationships which possess characteristics like those described above. It is true that the transference can be mostly sexual, but much of the work of a skilled group leader is in connection with sibling or mutual identification transference. Sibling transference is the process of reacting in the group as one did in his family of origin. Identification transference (universality—Yalom, 1975) refers to the awareness of the similarity of experiences, needs, and feelings which the group members have. This awareness can help an individual be more objective and encourage him to face and cope with his own difficulties. Identification transference is also the foundation for group unity during the negative phases of the transference toward the group leader (Slavson, 1950). When the transferences in the group are primarily sibling or identification, there are real possibilities for helping people develop themselves. I am of the opinion, though, that if the transference is primarily sexual (and very little of the basic transference is sibling or identification), the prognosis for a particular group member's being helped is poor. I think this opinion has validity for the following reasons:

(1) The more immature or underdeveloped a person is emotionally, mentally, and religiously, the less he can communicate on a deep intrapersonal and interpersonal level.

(2) The more immature one is, the more he tends to idealize, and the more likely he is to be sentimentally or erotically attracted to the group leader or other members of the group.

Although I have separated sexual, sibling, and identification transferences, it should be understood that they overlap and are interwoven to some degree in many transference relationships.

As a result of the various transferences that occur in the group situation, a group member is able to regress emotionally to an earlier state and safely re-experience early traumas and unconscious conflicts. This process is known as **catharsis**. Catharsis is most effective for an individual when it occurs on the verbal and emotional levels simultaneously. However, catharsis can occur only in a transference relationship because of the emotional setting in the group. This atmosphere favors bringing to consciousness suppressed and repressed guilt-evoking and anxiety-inducing feelings, thoughts, and strivings. One reason for **resisting uncovering repressed earlier feelings** is that these are chiefly of a **hostile** and **sexual** nature, and they tend to arouse **shame, guilt**, and **anxiety**. Furthermore, the **fear of regression** is one of the causes of negative transference, and catharsis cannot occur unless a person has the security which a positive transference assures.

Catharsis induces regression to stages at which emotional development (fixation) was arrested. It is necessary for a person to be free of fear and misgivings before he can allow himself to regress. In addition to the deeper psychological elements in one's resistance to regression, there is also the present factor of self-regard or pride. For example, the self-esteem of a particular group member receives a severe jolt when he confesses to impulses which make him feel debased, immoral, and anxious. It is very difficult to face these truths within oneself, and much more difficult to divulge them to others. In order for one to disclose his thoughts and feelings, he must give up some of his ego defenses. In order to do this effectively, a group member needs to feel assured that his guilt will not be further intensified through disdain, criticism, or punishment from the group leader (parental figure). A leader's attitude should be such that each group member is assured of being accepted and not ridiculed by the leader or group members. A group member needs this assurance because a religious leader symbolizes not only the parent, but society and God.

There are at least three advantages of the group's dealing with catharsis and regression:

(1) Resistance to regression is diminished through identification transferences. This happens because the members support each other and sanction aggression, especially toward the leader (parent). It is, therefore, easier to let down one's defenses and to regress when in an identification transference.

(2) Identification and universalization (realizing other group members are like me) reduce guilt, and the friendly atmosphere of the group makes it possible for group members to discharge hitherto hidden feelings and to break the dams that block the flow of their emotional and mental energies.

Resentment and hostility now can be **expressed** and dealt with responsibly.

(3) Group members re-enact their attitudes toward their parents, siblings, spouses, and other persons in relation to one another and toward the group leader. This re-enactment is particularly valuable to those with weak egos because it helps them overcome resistances and serves as a reality testing situation. Some group members who feel insecure and inadequate find it easier to act out than to verbalize their difficulties. Their acting out may take the form of aggression and rivalry.

Catharsis may give a person temporary relief, but **emotional maturity is achieved through insight** (Yalom, 1975). Helping an individual to achieve insight necessitates the group leader's distinguishing between interpretation and explanation. Explanation is a mental effort to establish the relation between cause and effect, and to give intellectual meaning to a phenomenon. Explanation deals largely with overt behavior and may ignore emotional factors. In group dynamics, emotions have ascendancy over reason and behavior. Therefore, in group conflict, the emotional elements are predominant. It is just not enough for a group member to analyze his problems and reactions intellectually; he must also process the emotions that accompany them (Horney, 1939; Slavson, 1950).

Mere **understanding**, then, cannot be relied on in a dynamic group, but well-timed interpretations can help a person to recognize the unconscious drives and strivings that motivate his behavior (Romans 7:15; Slavson, 1950, pp. 55, 56). It is important that a group member be ready to accept what the group leader says or what other members of the group say, and that he be able to recognize its relevance. In order to do this, it will be necessary to overcome some resistances and to establish a transference relationship; otherwise, an interpretation will be rejected or misunderstood. A group member must develop a degree of emotional maturity and ego strength before he can develop insight and accept interpretation. Jesus talked about the importance of readiness when He said, "I have much more to say to you, more than you can now bear" (John 16:12; see also John 6:60).

An interpretation should be profitable and not harmful. But for an interpretation to be therapeutic, there are two questions which a leader should keep in mind:

(1) Can a group member stand a particular insight at this time?

(2) Is an interpretation likely to have meaning for him in that perhaps it will start him thinking in a constructive way? (Horney, 1939, pp. 222, 223). A fair rule of thumb is: give an interpretation when a particular group member is at the point where he can almost formulate it himself (Slavson, 1950, p. 56).

There are some difficulties regarding interpretations in groups that are not encountered in individual situations, and perhaps **readiness** is the most difficult factor. One cannot assume that all group members have worked through repressions and have overcome resistances at the same rate. Therefore, an interpretation that is well-timed for one person may be out of place for others (Slavson, 1950, p. 56).

An Effective Leader Analyzes Resistance and Transference

A group member's relationship patterns with his family members and with other people are reproduced in the group, and the leader should be alert to these reproductions. Through group interaction, a leader should encourage the person's awareness of what he does and should lead the individual toward constructive change.

Many children grow up with unresolved feelings of hostility toward their parents. They find it difficult to outgrow rebellion against parental authority. They think parents try to make them change their ways or pressure them to conform to parental standards. Some individuals transfer these feelings to the group leader because they are being encouraged to discard old personality patterns for new ones. This form of **resistance** must be worked through by exploring the relationship with the parents, and resolving the factors of irrational rebellion born in childhood and still lingering in the present (Durkin, 1964). Each group member must learn to differentiate unhealthy resistance to change from constructive freedom and adult independence.

When group members have a positive relationship with their leader and feel respect and admiration for him, they will tend to absorb many of his characteristics. These qualities come through by verbal and nonverbal communication. The group members observe closely the leader's appearance, his handling of a crisis, his language, his fairness, and his sense of humor. If there is a gap between the leader and members of the group in terms of age, class, education, race, or ethnic identity, there also could be an underlying distrust and hostility which, if not faced and resolved, would retard the growth of the individual. However, the timing is important, because a person will not allow himself to explore these conflicts until he feels ready, and until the relationship with the leader has reached a solid basis (Becker, 1972).

A group member may distort the relationship with the leader because of the group member's conflicting needs. A leader must not provide him a real basis, though, for negative or destructive reaction. A group leader must be warm, friendly, and fair, but also firm. Since people suffer from considerable hopelessness and pessimism, they have a great need for constructive inspiration which is experienced through the leader's personality. It is most helpful for the member of the group to believe that the leader has skill, experience, knowledge, and maturity. The group members look to the leader for guidance, but they tend also to distort the extent of his ability. Either they magnify his powers and expect miraculous help, or they may reject his help and feel hostile toward him. Also, they often project their self-doubts and self-rejection onto the leader and feel he is being hostile to them.

A group leader must see and hear not only intellectual ideas or concepts, but also such feelings as anger, guilt, shame, fear, depression, insecurity, and inadequacy which a group member may be expressing through nonverbal communication. A group member communicates nonverbally through such dynamics as change in posture, speech rate, tone of voice, facial expressions, and gestures. A leader should also see and hear if a group member is trying to cover up or deny, perhaps unconsciously, his feelings of anger, shame, guilt, insecurity, and inadequacy by being arrogant, defensive, and rigid. In addition, a group member may use denial by focusing on others and their mistakes and weaknesses. These are forms of **resistance** to change, and an effective leader sees, hears, and feels the resistance.

Resistance should be seen as a natural force which is experienced by individuals or the group as a body. Therefore, when one is resisting, he should not be viewed as **bad**. Furthermore, it needs to be understood that resistance takes place on both a conscious and an unconscious level. While it is the group member's desire to change, there is also a struggle not to change. Resistance is that force which seeks to maintain a balance within the individual or group. A leader should not avoid resistance but focus on it by calling attention verbally and nonverbally to it. A leader also effectively responds to it through joining the individual doing the resisting. He may join by confronting the resistance as Jesus suggested: "Settle matters quickly with your adversary who is taking you to court. Do it while you are still with him on the way, or he may hand you over to the judge, and the judge may hand you over to the officer, and you may be thrown into prison" (Matthew 5:25). A person who is resisting tends to see the leader or a group member as an adversary. A leader is ineffective when viewed by a group member as being in an adversarial position.

A person may claim he wants to change, and yet be afraid to change. He may feel his own personality integration is in a state of fragile equilibrium. He may have a deep fear of losing his only known solutions to his problems of living. His patterns have been learned over many years and, although they may be unhealthy and impoverishing, they may afford him personal gratifications which he doubts he could obtain in any other way.

The fear of change is associated with pessimistic, resigned, hopeless feelings about oneself. An individual may be afraid that he does not have the resources to grow, to take responsibility, and to develop himself. Therefore, he may cling to ineffective solutions to his problems and personal growth. The resistance to change may be seen as the result of self-hate, defeatism, and self-rejection. This person has a **despised** as well as an **idealized** image of himself. If he too strongly identifies with his despised image, not only does he lack faith in his constructive resources, but he also feels hopelessness that he could ever achieve his potential. Furthermore, the self-hate leads to a desire to hurt oneself rather than to promote one's growth and welfare.

There are also specific resistances which occur in the group because of the multiplicity of group relationships. Although when people come together they can be immensely stimulating to one another, they are also guarded and distrustful. The more cohesive the group and the warmer the group atmosphere, the less defensive will group members become. People generally maintain a facade in their relationships with others.

In defining group cohesion, Kellerman (1981, pp. 256, 257) says:

> *My definition of* **group cohesion** *would include the following: the psychological state which enables a collection of people to experience a unity of feeling and purpose and to work in harmony toward a common goal. This would be in contrast to a state we might call* **group adhesion** *in which people experience a unity of purpose but do not put that unity into common action. The adhesive team does everything together but does not play well together on the field. The adhesive therapy group loves its leader but does not succeed in helping to change its members' lives. A family can certainly be adhesive in its demands for loyalty and obedience but not necessarily cohesive in its unity of purpose.*

For some people, closeness with others is a warm, attractive experience. Group members who are particularly detached find closeness in the group threatening to them. In fact, they may actually leave the group or, if they remain, they will put up defenses which preserve distances between them and the other group members. In the severely detached person, this can become a difficult technical problem, and the untrained leader can be hurtful. The group can have a compelling and constructive influence on the detached person if he remains in the group, and thus help him to break through his detachment. This problem is worked through not only by exploring the dynamics of detachment, but by repeated interactions with other members of the group.

There are other forms of resistance, such as the following:

(1) Being late to various meetings.

(2) Denying the reality of one's problems.

(3) Appearing to solve one's problems too quickly; for example, thinking a deep-seated and long-standing conflict can be settled with a simple apology.

(4) Being silent.

(5) Being too polite or overly friendly.

(6) Being too agreeable.

(7) Blaming others.

(8) Being cynical.

(9) Hostile verbalizing, such as criticisms of the leader and his classroom setup or quoting other **authorities** to the effect that groups are **bad**.

(10) Monopolizing the time.

(11) Intellectualizing—talking to avoid feeling.

It is much easier to **deny or to talk around** resistance than it is to confront it. Individual and group growth is contingent upon a number of factors. Two central factors are the **resistances** and **transferences** which **will emerge** in the group and which must be analyzed. Resistance takes many forms in a group. One of the most difficult ones to deal with is that of resisting transference analysis. It should be understood that resistance and transference are two very powerful forces, and thus have powerful influences in the group. Resistance and transference are so powerful that they are central to both the group's numerical and internal growth and to its degeneration and death. **Remember**, in a group, **that which is resisted** is that which **will persist unless analyzed and processed.**

An Effective Leader Sees the Group as a Recapitulation of One's Family

As mentioned in chapter one, a person becomes a member of a group because he is trying to meet certain needs. Some of his needs may be unconscious. One paradoxical need he has is that of leaving his family of origin on the one hand and finding it on the other hand. The group to which one belongs (belonging necessitates emotional bonding) recapitulates his family of origin. If a group influences one in a growth direction, the group member will experience a corrective emotional recapitulation of his primary family group (Yalom, 1975). If one's commitment (which may be unconscious) is to remain emotionally or physically with one's family of origin, then he will not desire and, therefore, will not be deeply involved in a group whose purpose is to allow him to have a corrective emotional experience. If one's commitment is to **leave home**, he will seek a group which will recapitulate his family of origin and provide for him a corrective emotional experience.

A corrective emotional experience is one which is similar to a past experience. In the initial experience, one was hurt through being ridiculed or frightened or harshly judged. In the current experience, the group member has similar feelings, but other group members do not ridicule, frighten, or harshly judge. **Experiencing this emotional difference is what corrects and heals.** Therefore, given enough of these experiences, one not only works through the trauma of past experiences but, in a similar future situation, does not expect the reaction from others to be like the initial reaction. For example, if one grew up with very judgmental parents, he will expect authority figures to be judgmental. However, given enough experiences with a nonjudgmental leader, a person can reach the point where he does not automatically expect authority figures to be judgmental of him.

Many congregations are made up primarily of two or three (nuclear and extended) families. Those congregations may not allow corrective experiences to take place because they do not want their members to leave their families of origin. An individual who does not want to leave home emotionally or physically may identify with the congregation where his family attends. Congregations of this type can tolerate few members who are not part of the extended family. They are so determined to keep their families intact that they are not open to new members becoming a part of the congregation. This is not often explicitly stated, but usually it is an unwritten rule of which the group member may not be aware. Thus, those individuals who become members of this type of group and remain are not wanting to leave home. They simply are trying to remain symbolically with their families of origin.

An individual who, for whatever reasons, is geographically separated from his immediate family will seek a group which recapitulates his family of origin. If his desire is not to leave home, he will search for a group which will relate to him dynamically the way he was related to in his family of origin. If a person had a narrow-minded and arrogant father, he will tend to find a congregation where the leaders are narrow-minded and arrogant. If his family of origin was filled with parental fighting and sibling rivalry, he will tend to find a congregation which has considerable fighting between the leaders and among the group members.

A person who wishes consciously or unconsciously to leave home, when geographically separated from his family of origin, will seek a group which not only recapitulates his primary family, but which will provide him some of the corrective experiences which are necessary for leaving home. This is just as true with religious groups as with any social group. An individual who has a deep-seated need to leave home, if geographically separated from his family, will, in the process of growing up, tend to find different church groups which will provide him the corrective emotional experiences. Enough such experiences will help one to leave home emotionally.

This idea should not be thought strange because individuals often use expressions such as "this is my home away from home" or "my church family." One commonly hears individuals referring to the leaders or members as being good parents, or certain persons remind them of an uncle, aunt, brother, or sister. Individuals may just as frequently see leaders and group members as representing a parent, sibling, or other relative who caused them pain while growing up. There may be times when individuals are not aware of why other group members irritate, frighten, or embarrass them. The roots of such feelings most likely lie in one's nuclear or extended family. Anger at an elder, minister, or Bible teacher may have its roots in unresolved anger toward one's parents. Fights over who is in control also may be rooted in unresolved authority issues in one's childhood. Stress on what should and should not be done by group members is a way of avoiding intimacy of which the group is afraid.

A Challenge To Christian Leaders

As long as leaders do not understand the powerful forces of church conflict and do not learn how to manage them effectively, the forces in church conflict will continue to disrupt church growth, splinter and divide Christians, and reinforce the fear of conflict itself. As long as the **fear of conflict controls the leadership**, the members of the body of Christ will experience the severe, and in many cases, terminal pain of unmanaged church conflict. As long as church leaders attempt to prevent and resolve **people conflict** through **"quarreling about words"** (2 Timothy 2:14,23; Titus 3:9-11) instead of focusing on the intrapersonal, interpersonal, and objective dimensions of their conflict (p. 19), church conflict can neither be effectively managed nor resolved. **But**, when church leaders accept their fear of conflict and learn how to confront their fear instead of denying it, church conflict can be an opportunity for growth.

Growth through conflict becomes a reality when group theory is understood and applied to the church family. Only then can it be more effectively managed. This insight into group theory gives leaders a stable footing which is necessary if the dynamics of conflict are to be channeled into creativity and not into degeneration and destruction of the group.

Conflict has been, is, and will be in the church family, but group theory understood and effectively applied can enable the church to grow through its conflict.

References

Allport, G. W., **The Individual and His Religion** (New York: Macmillan, 1950).

Becker, B. J., "The Psychodynamics of Analytic Group Psychotherapy," **The American Journal of Psychoanalysis**, 1972, 32(2), 180.

Durkin, H. E., **The Group in Depth** (5th edition) (New York: International Universities Press, Inc., 1973).

Horney, K., **New Ways in Psychoanalysis** (New York: W. W. Norton, 1966).

Kellerman, H., **Group Cohesion: Theoretical and Clinical Perspectives** (New York: Grune & Stratton, 1981).

Slavson, S. R., **Analytic Group Psychotherapy** (New York: Columbia University Press, 1950).

Yalom, I. D., **The Theory and Practice of Group Psychotherapy** (New York: Basic Books, 1975).